KILLING THE GAME

The inside story behind the transformation of Manchester City and the creation of City Football Group

DANIEL SLACK-SMITH

ABOUT
THIS BOOK

This is the inside story behind the transformation of Manchester City since September 2008 and the creation of City Football Group, that now owns stakes in six clubs on five continents, from the perspective of the key decision-makers that have been involved in this groundbreaking project.

It is largely based on a series of exclusive interviews with more than 50 current and former officials of Manchester City, City Football Group, and Abu Dhabi United Group, among others, that were conducted in the UK, US, Australia and the UAE over the last two years.

The author was also granted unprecedented access to a wide variety of contemporaneous documents, records, trails of correspondence and other materials related to the City project over the last ten years, in order to gain a better understanding of how and why things happened the way they did.

That explains what this book is. It's important to be clear about what it is not.

It isn't entirely objective. It is based on interviews with people that believe in the City project and have been involved in its planning and execution. The author has been a long-term advisor to Abu Dhabi United Group. Third party critics don't get equal time on these pages.

It isn't nostalgic. It zooms in on the last ten years of a story that began in 1894, and makes no attempt to document the eventful decades at Manchester City that immediately preceded the Abu Dhabi United Group takeover. Others are more qualified to render that period of the Club's history with the authenticity it deserves, and indeed many have done so.

It isn't exhaustive. It focuses on the views and recollections of a limited group of senior decision-makers, and does not feature the countless other people that have contributed in both small and large ways to the success of the City project over the last ten years, including most notably, the employees and supporters of Manchester City and its sister clubs.

Readers are therefore invited to apply whatever filters they choose to the narrative that follows. This is one version of one part of the story. The one that is told inside the walls of the City Football Academy, Manchester, and in City Football Group offices around the world.

I would like to thank everybody that agreed to be interviewed for this project. It's been a privilege to rummage around in your memories in order to tell this remarkable story.

Daniel Slack-Smith
August 2018

FOREWORD
BY MIKE SUMMERBEE

I write this foreword with great pride and a little trepidation. As a former player in the 1960s and 70s Manchester City has been in my heart, and been a major part of my life, for a long time.

I hope my attempts to commit a few of my thoughts to paper can do justice to the hard work, dedication, and vision that have revolutionised this great football club.

Everything has come together so spectacularly, and with such fantastic results on and off the pitch over the past decade, that sometimes I must pinch myself. However, none of it has been by accident or through luck.

When HH Sheikh Mansour bought City back in September 2008, he purchased a club with heart, with soul, with history and tradition but one that was admittedly a little frayed around the edges. It had a loyal fanbase which was buoyed only by their enduring love and gallows humour. Glorious, sometimes comedic, failure was scattered through the previous, trophy-free, thirty-plus years.

A decade on and the perception of the Club worldwide has been transformed, the psyche of those supporters rehabilitated but the character preserved. The heart beats loudly and the soul is well-nourished, and we clearly have Sheikh Mansour, our chairman Khaldoon Al Mubarak and the board and staff to thank for that.

Having played for City in a golden era when domestic and European trophies were won, it had long been my wish that new heroes, decorated in medals, would emerge. Thankfully the names of Bell, Lee and Summerbee have been supplanted. New legends have been and are being created, new heights being scaled, and new records being set by the dozen.

Seeing how Manchester City has been transformed over the past ten years gladdens my heart and makes it swell with pride.

The Club, its immediate neighbourhood and the conditions for the hard-working staff that keep it all ticking along, have been improved beyond anyone's wildest dreams. The partnerships with the community and with the local council are strong and purposeful and have also benefitted from far-sightedness and careful planning and crucially, the family feel of this Club has been cherished and maintained.

Many, many, times since 2008 there were fans of other clubs and the merely uninformed telling me the ownership would get bored, that it wouldn't or couldn't last. Manchester City, they said, was a plaything that would be cast aside, traditions lost or forgotten. How wrong they all were.

Manchester City is thriving, the traditions are as strong as ever and the future is so exciting.

In these pages, you will meet some of the central characters of the latest chapters of City's great history. You will be privy to the guiding principles, never-before publicised insights and discover the truth behind myths and stories.

This is a book, which I believe captures the full-spirited nature of the modern Manchester City and re-affirms everything that this Club has stood for in its 124 years and why even our biggest rivals admire what has been done and the facilities that have been put in place.

For someone who has been associated with this club as a player, ambassador and above all supporter for more than 50 years, I cannot express how enjoyable the last ten years have been and to be involved now in something like this is something very special for me and for all the ex-players that the Club looks after so well.

What we see in and around the Etihad Stadium today has all been created by quality; not only quality of players and managers but the quality of its leadership and its vision. I am firmly of the view, as I believe the pages that follow demonstrate, that Manchester City has never been in better hands.

Enjoy the journey.

CONTENTS

WHO'S WHO

His Highness Sheikh Mansour bin Zayed Al Nahyan
Owner of Manchester City and City Football Group [CFG] through private investment company, Abu Dhabi United Group [ADUG]

Khaldoon Al Mubarak
Chairman of Manchester City and CFG

Chris Bailey
Editor-in-Chief at Manchester City

Gareth Barry
Former England international and Manchester City player from 2009 to 2013

Txiki Begiristain
Former Spain international and now Football Director at Manchester City

Sir Howard Bernstein
Chief Executive of Manchester City Council from 1998 to 2017 and now an advisor to ADUG.

Omar Berrada
Manchester City's Chief Operating Officer

Pete Bradshaw
Manchester City's Director of Infrastructure & Estates

Simon Cliff
General Counsel of CFG

Garry Cook
Executive Chairman of Manchester City at the time of the ADUG takeover then CEO of Manchester City until September 2011

Don Dransfield
Director of Operations Development at CFG

Marty Edelman
Board director of Manchester City and CFG and Vice Chairman of New York City FC

Tom Glick
Chief Commercial Officer of CFG who served as President of New York City FC from January 2015 to March 2016

Pep Guardiola
Manager of Manchester City since 2016, former manager of FC Barcelona and Bayern Munich

Gary James
Historian/lecturer of sport and Manchester City Museum & Tour project manager from 2002 to 2009

Steph Houghton
England international and Captain of Manchester City's women's team since 2014

Brian Kidd
Former England international, former player and coach at both Manchester City and Manchester United, and Assistant Coach at Manchester City under Roberto Mancini, Manuel Pellegrini and Pep Guardiola

Vicky Kloss
Chief Communications Officer for CFG

Vincent Kompany
Belgian international and Captain of Manchester City who joined the Club shortly before the ADUG takeover in 2008

Joleon Lescott
Former England international and Manchester City player from 2009 to 2014

Randy Levine
President of the New York Yankees, which owns a minority stake in New York City FC through Yankee Global Enterprises

John MacBeath
Board director of Manchester City and CFG and interim CEO of Manchester City from September 2011 to August 2012.

Tommy McNamara
New York City FC player since the Club's inaugural season in 2015

Roberto Mancini
Manager of Manchester City from December 2009 to May 2013

Brian Marwood
Former England international, now Head of Global Football at CFG, and formerly Manchester City's Chief Football Administration Officer from 2009 to 2012

Scott Munn
CEO of Melbourne City FC

Simon Pearce
Board director of Manchester City and CFG and Vice Chairman of Melbourne City FC

Manuel Pellegrini
Manager of Manchester City from June 2013 to June 2016

Claudio Reyna
Former US international and Manchester City player from 2003 to 2007, and now Sporting Director of New York City FC

Ferran Soriano
CEO of Manchester City and CFG

Jon Stemp
Long-term infrastructure advisor to Manchester City and CFG

Mike Summerbee
Former England international and Manchester City player from 1965 to 1975, and a Club Ambassador since 2009

Yaya Touré
Ivory Coast international and Manchester City player from 2010 to 2018

Patrick Vieira
Former French international who played at Manchester City from 2009 to 2011. After his retirement, Vieira joined Manchester City as an executive before coaching its Elite Development Squad. He then served as Head Coach of New York City FC from January 2016 to June 2018

David Villa
Former Spain international and Captain of New York City FC since the Club's inaugural season in 2015

Jason Wilcox
Former England international and now Academy Director at Manchester City

Danny Wilson
Operations Director at Manchester City

MANCHESTER CITY

SEPTEMBER 2008 TO MAY 2013

CHAPTER 1:
DEADLINE DAY

| MANCHESTER, ENGLAND |

On the morning of 1 September 2008, Gary James arrived at the City of Manchester Stadium shortly after 8am. A football historian and lifelong Manchester City supporter, he worked part-time as a consultant to the Club and curated a museum at the Stadium.

"I got in," remembers James, "and then somebody else arrived and said, 'Have you heard this rumour? We're going to sign [then Newcastle United striker] Michael Owen!'"

"Nah, that's rubbish," replied James.

Before the rise of fake news, there had always been transfer deadline day.

"Then they said, 'But we're also selling [Vedran] Ćorluka,'" recalls James, "and that was really bad news, right? Not because of anything special about the player, but it was like, 'Ah, typical... we're selling someone we need.'"

By chance, James had a meeting on his calendar that morning with Manchester City's Executive Chairman, Garry Cook, to discuss some potential improvements to the museum. Cook was late, so James waited outside his office.

"I am waiting," remembers James, "and then all of a sudden he came bouncing in,

'Gaz, we've got to call it off. Something's happening. You're going to love it. I can't say what it is, but you're going to love it."'

Cook was always energetic, but James says this morning was different.

"It was the most animated I'd ever seen him," he says. "It was like a kid in a sweet shop it was, and he'd never called me 'Gaz' before."

By the time James had returned to his desk, the story had taken on a whole new dimension.

"I got back to the office, and one of the other guys said, 'This Michael Owen rumour's getting stronger, and apparently we are being taken over."'

The takeover subplot had a familiar ring to it. Manchester City had been acquired by foreign owners [UK Sports Investments, led by former Thai Prime Minister, Thaksin Shinawatra] less than 15 months earlier.

James recounted to his colleagues the unusual encounter that he had just had with the ebullient Cook.

"I said, 'Garry Cook,'" recalls James, "he called me 'Gaz,' and he cancelled our meeting because something is going to happen that I am going to love.'"

It wasn't confirmed, but they were convinced.

"Well," said James, processing it all. "Apparently, we've been taken over."

| LONDON, ENGLAND |

Simon Cliff, then a young associate in the London office of international law firm, Shearman & Sterling, rode the London Underground to work that morning just like any other. As he alighted at Kings Cross station, he had no idea how much his life was about to change.

"I got to work and Laurence Levy [partner at Shearman & Sterling] grabbed me," says Cliff. "As I recall it, he had just spent the weekend working on the Manchester City deal, after having been brought in at the end of the previous week on this MOU."

The MOU [Memorandum of Understanding], signed at the Emirates Palace Hotel in Abu Dhabi on 31 August 2008, mapped out the terms for the proposed sale of

90% of Manchester City from Thaksin Shinawatra's UK Sports Investments, to Abu Dhabi United Group [ADUG], owned by His Highness Sheikh Mansour bin Zayed Al Nahyan. The job of the lawyers, including Cliff, was to convert that MOU into a contract of sale.

"The legal analysis would be that the MOU was always subject to contract," explains Cliff, "so it was an agreement to do the deal, but the deal still needed to be done. His Highness [Sheikh Mansour] did not own shares in the Club, and there were no binding contracts in place. There was just this loose MOU, together with the fact that he had also loaned the Club, I think it was the best part of £30 to £35 million."

According to Cliff, this wasn't how transactions on this scale were generally conducted, although it wasn't unheard of.

"The MOU was a page-and-a-half committing someone to pay a nine-figure sum for a football club," he says, "which is probably not where most lawyers feel comfortable."

Cliff and his colleagues were given a week to turn the non-binding MOU into a legally-binding contract for the sale of Manchester City.

It would take them three, and the final agreement would come in at over a hundred pages.

| ABU DHABI, UAE |

Simon Pearce's office sat at the end of a long corridor on the 9th floor of the recently-completed Al Mamoura office building. As the head of Strategic Communications for the Government of Abu Dhabi, his job was to protect and enhance the reputation of the Emirate of Abu Dhabi in the eyes of the world. He had a large television bolted to the wall beside his desk which was always on at a low volume while he worked.

It was a small news item running along the bottom of that screen that first alerted Pearce that an investor from Abu Dhabi had been linked to the purchase of Manchester City. The news got his attention. In the preceding years, Pearce had been involved in a number of high-profile international investments emanating from the Emirate, and knew just how carefully the communications around these transactions had to be managed. A ticker headline that raised more questions than it answered was not an ideal place to start.

"We all got ambushed by it because we just didn't know who was behind it," says Pearce. "I had just been involved in the development of the brand of Abu Dhabi [which had emphasised the Emirate's understated style], and then this petro-dollar cliché suddenly comes up on three different news services at once, and my first reaction was, 'What the hell is going on?'"

Pearce turned up the volume on his television and began investigating the story in the UAE.

| MANCHESTER, ENGLAND |

Vicky Kloss, then Manchester City's Head of Communications, was also taken by surprise. Cook had alerted her during the previous week that the Club was potentially for sale, and that a wealthy investor had shown some interest, but not that a takeover was imminent.

"It started with a phone call from a journalist from Bloomberg," says Kloss, "who had picked up on a story on ArabianBusiness.com that a company in Abu Dhabi was going to buy Manchester City."

As Kloss set out to confirm whether the initial report was accurate, the sudden emergence of an enthusiastic spokesperson for the new investor quickly sent the story into overdrive.

"Before we knew it we had a guy called Sulaiman Al Fahim, a self-appointed spokesperson for the Abu Dhabi United Group, appearing on every television and radio station by mid-morning," recalls Kloss.

"Nobody could get a hold of Sulaiman Al Fahim," recalls Cook, "but he was giving the media his mobile phone number, which was bizarre."

Al Fahim – who had been involved behind-the-scenes in the brokering of the deal – boasted in interviews of ADUG's wealth, raised the prospect of Manchester City winning the UEFA Champions League, and rattled off a provocative list of high-profile transfer targets. It made for great copy but was a fairly brash introduction to the global football media and the British public.

"Let's face it," says Kloss, "everybody knows that the first interview, the first appearance, the first event, whatever it may be, is so critical because it sets the tone going forward, and this was pretty catastrophic in that respect. And whilst he wasn't doing anything with malice, and was probably enjoying his moment, and the media were certainly enjoying it, and our fans were sort of enjoying it, you had this other swathe of the population who were looking at it with utter distaste."

After speaking with Cook and huddling with the Club's lawyers, Kloss issued a two-sentence statement at 12.08pm intended to calm things down:

"Manchester City can confirm that a Memorandum of Understanding has been signed between the Abu Dhabi United Group and Manchester City Football Club Limited. A period of due diligence for all parties, including the FA Premier League, has now been entered."

The statement was neat and precise, and made clear that the deal wasn't done. However, its sobering impact was swamped by the loquacious Al Fahim, by now being described in a range of media outlets as 'the Donald Trump' of the Arab World [having hosted a reality show in the UAE, The Hydra Executives, which bore more than a passing resemblance to The Apprentice].

In a page that could have been lifted straight out of the Trump playbook, the original story on ArabianBusiness.com that had set off the global firestorm framed the deal as "a great coup for Al Fahim" and lauded him – the only person quoted in the piece – as "the successful architect of the deal."[1]

"Now what was happening," says Kloss, "is that with all those incredible quotes from this magnetic character, and the joy that the British media were receiving him with, because he was just fabulous fodder for them, it meant that by this point Manchester City fans were gathering outside the Stadium, literally with tea towels on their heads, imitating Arab dress. It really was the most insane day in British football."

"The world had exploded," says Cook. "It was like a volcano had just erupted and, what we were not doing in the euphoria, is we were probably not paying attention to managing the process of communicating. It was all out of our hands. We were just doing our best with what we had. We were really in the midst of a storm and Vicky, who we all had the greatest respect for, was like, 'Stop the madness. We have got to stop the madness. We have got to calm this down.'"

At the offices of Manchester City, at that time housed in the City of Manchester Stadium [now Etihad Stadium], the Club's employees didn't down tools completely, but the news was never far from their minds.

"You were forever kind of doing your work and then looking up at Sky Sports News and seeing what was going on," says Danny Wilson, then Head of Supporter Experience at Manchester City. "And then you start to see people arriving on the site, you get camera crews arriving at the Stadium and using it as a backdrop, and you are thinking, 'Actually, I am just behind there. This is being played out to global media, and that is where my office is.'"

"The entire staff at the Club were excited because all of a sudden people were paying attention to us," says Cook. "We had never had that attention. You have to put it into context that Manchester United had hogged all of the media attention, and we had not been a part of any of it."

As the drama continued to unfold, Manchester City staff watched on with a mix of hope and trepidation.

"It was kind of double-edged, really," says Wilson. "There was the excitement of what this could bring, and what it could mean, but also apprehension and concern that it could mean something negative. That they are going to bring in all new people, and take the Club in a direction that isn't where this football club should be, and what it was founded on, and all of that could crumble and break."

Wilson comes across in person as anything but a pessimist, but the Club's recent experience with foreign ownership had been mixed.

"We had just been through a period of change prior to that, under Thaksin Shinawatra, which was interesting in different ways," he says, "but it took us into a space where the football club probably became something that it wasn't, and hadn't ever been before."

In the final hour of the transfer window, the signing of the Brazilian striker, Robinho, for £32.5m, added a final dose of drama to one of the most dramatic days in the history of Manchester City.

"We got him on a private plane," says Cook, recalling the frantic rush to get the deal done before the transfer window closed. "There were lots of issues back in those days where registration paperwork used to arrive by fax at Premier League offices after midnight, and because of that they brought in a regulation that if it is not in by midnight, it is not there. I remember saying to Dave Richards [then Chairman of the

Premier League], 'Dave, the paperwork is coming! Honestly, it is coming,' concerned that we would miss the deadline on such a milestone transaction."

"It was fantastic," then Club Secretary Bernard Halford told The Telegraph's Mark Ogden in 2011. "We signed Robinho at the last minute and I remember having to get the forms done at ten to midnight and all the fans were outside, driving around the stadium, beeping their horns and singing."[2]

It was a positive note to end on, but according to Kloss, who burned through four mobile phone batteries on that one chaotic day, the takeover spectacle left an impression in the minds of many that would taint their perceptions of Manchester City and its owner for years to come.

"It was a very difficult start," she says. "As a lifelong City fan, I was half excited and half sceptical, but from a communications point of view, it was a nightmare, and there are still ramifications of that to this day. We still have those that go, you know, 'This is just the rich, oil, Arab, plaything, and you don't act with class.' So yes, how not to announce your arrival, really, was September the 1st, 2008."

Sulaiman Al Fahim would go on to play no role in the ownership of Manchester City. He would briefly resurface in the UK in 2009 as the new owner of Portsmouth FC and in February 2018 would reportedly be sentenced to five years in prison in the UAE for bank fraud related to the financing of that transaction.

| ABU DHABI, UAE |

Khaldoon Al Mubarak knew right away that the mystery investor behind ADUG was His Highness Sheikh Mansour bin Zayed Al Nahyan.

A half-brother to the UAE President and full-brother to the Crown Prince of Abu Dhabi, Sheikh Mansour was already a powerful figure in business, government and sports in the UAE that had only months earlier made an unusually high-profile investment in Barclays. His late father, Sheikh Zayed bin Sultan Al Nahyan, was the beloved former Ruler of Abu Dhabi and founding President of the UAE.

"Sheikh Mansour had told me months earlier of his intention to buy a Premier League club," says Al Mubarak, who already knew the young Sheikh well.

Sheikh Mansour had then tapped Al Mubarak – a knowledgeable football fan and experienced international investor as the CEO of Mubadala – for his topline thoughts on a number of potential acquisition targets in the months before the move for Manchester City.

"He had a couple of people looking after that [the search for a club]," explains Al Mubarak, "and every time a real option would come in, he would give me a call and say 'What do you think?'"

According to those with knowledge of the deliberations, Sheikh Mansour and his advisors had run their ruler over at least three Premier League clubs in addition to Manchester City. A secret meeting had even taken place in a Paris hotel room with a senior figure from one major London-based club to discuss a potential deal.

"By the beginning of that summer [2008]," says Mubarak, "it was clear Sheikh Mansour had zoomed in on Manchester City as the most attractive proposition. And then he proceeded. He did the deal."

The Sheikh's deal was global news overnight. The announcement was quickly amplified by the bullish comments of front man, Sulaiman Al Fahim, on the supercharged final day of the transfer window.

Al Mubarak is diplomatic when the topic of Al Fahim comes up.

"I mean, listen," he says, "Sulaiman Al Fahim essentially acted as a broker. He was there in that initial phase, brokering the deal, and then he became the centre of the storm."

Although it is hard to imagine Al Mubarak engaging in such loose talk himself, the day's events left him in no doubt about the combustible nature of the media landscape around the Premier League.

"It was kind of a big wake up call," he says, having monitored the frenzy from a distance. "I was always a fan of football, and I think I'm pretty connected from a communications perspective, but I didn't anticipate the level of drama that you could see from the beginning. It was like, we've got to handle this carefully, because this thing could easily go out of control."

It was late on transfer deadline day when Sheikh Mansour asked Al Mubarak to personally oversee the completion of the deal. It isn't clear what impact, if any, the day's media coverage may have had on that decision. It is reasonable to speculate that the call may have come in anyway. Only one person knows for sure.

"Bear in mind," stresses Al Mubarak, "at that point, His Highness Sheikh Mansour hadn't decided how to manage this, or how to run this. The focus was on the transaction, not on the execution and the management. Once there was a principal understanding, and then once that explosion happened, that's when he asked me to step in. He asked me to close the deal out, negotiate it for the best possible outcome, and then once that's done, to manage the Club on his behalf, and be the Chairman."

| MANCHESTER, ENGLAND |

Gary James left work early on 1 September 2008.

"I had to go and pick my Dad up," he explains. "He was coming out of the hospital and I was collecting him and taking him home."

James's father is a diehard City supporter. He had carried his son to his first game at Maine Rd when Gary was only a baby, born during the historic 1967-68 season in which Manchester City had last won the League.

By the time James got in his car that afternoon, the takeover had been confirmed and BBC Radio 5 Live was awash with speculation about Manchester City's wealthy new owner.

"It had gone from 'City might be signing Michael Owen' to 'They're signing Berbatov,' and then 'They are signing Berbatov, and this bloke apparently has got more money than anyone else in the world,'" recalls James.

When he arrived at his destination, the historian was faced with a dilemma.

"I got to the hospital," recalls James, "and my Dad had been in because he had heart problems. I'd been listening to all this excitement, and I was thinking, this is like winning the FA Cup, it's like winning the League, and I was thinking, I can't tell me Dad because of his heart!"

He needn't have worried.

"I got to his ward and the first thing he said to me is, 'Have you heard?! Have you heard?!'" recalls a laughing James.

"It was like the best tonic he could have had."

CHAPTER 2:

OVERDUE DILIGENCE

Vincent Kompany signed a four-year deal with Manchester City just over a week before the proposed ADUG takeover was announced.

"It was a weird experience in general," he says of that time. "Pablo Zabaleta signed [on 31 August 2008] but like me, he was not necessarily the marquee signing of the moment. [Former City player] Shaun Wright-Phillips had come back, and at that time he was an absolute legend for the Club and the fans loved him, so that was the biggest move that City was able to do at that time."

Everything changed on 1 September 2008.

"Then they just came in with Robinho and blew everybody out of the water," says Kompany. "We didn't believe it at first. Then he turned up and, all of a sudden, we had Robinho."

For new signings such as Robinho, Kompany and Zabaleta, their first impressions of Manchester City were largely shaped by the dilapidated state of the Club's training ground in Carrington, a small village on the outskirts of Greater Manchester.

"I signed my contract before I saw the training ground," recalls Kompany, who completed his paperwork in the presence of Bernard Halford, who had served as Manchester City's Club Secretary since 1972, in an office piled high with boxes in the City of Manchester Stadium [now Etihad Stadium].

"They would drive you out when you signed your contract, but not before!" he adds with a laugh.

Manchester City players from that period speak about Carrington with a mix of nostalgia and disbelief that a Premier League side actually trained there.

"I remember going to the toilet for the first time," says Kompany, "and it was two cubicles, and one had a door, and the other one had the door hanging off almost. I thought, that's pretty interesting in term of intimacy. There was a machine with weights, where you couldn't really lift it, because there was so much rust on it. If you had a gym session, you'd always be at your maximum, because just to move that one little weight you first had to go through all the rust. There was a punching bag, that was half cut through the middle as if someone came in with a samurai sword. You had one glove to punch it, so you could develop an anomaly on one side from working out that way."

Kompany isn't done.

"And it was cold," he adds.

According to Yaya Touré, who would join Manchester City from FC Barcelona in 2010 [after more than £500k had been spent on upgrades to the Carrington facility], the state of the training ground was at odds with the Club's aspirations.

"Carrington was looking like a second division facility," says Touré. "In the beginning, I was complaining, to be honest. I was really concerned about it. At first, when I finished training, sometimes I didn't take a shower there, because I was not feeling myself, you know, and I wanted things to change."

The midfielder was particularly struck by the sight of horses wandering past the training ground.

"It was quite funny," he says, looking back. "I remember I told my brother [then Manchester City defender, Kolo Touré], 'The Club wants to achieve things. Why is it like this? Things have to change. We have to be serious.'"

Despite its shortcomings, Kompany maintains that Carrington still had its strengths.

"The pitches were immaculate," he says. "I remember the quality of the pitch, because a lot of teams, they've got it the other way around. They've got good infrastructure but they've got bad pitches. And if you start from the fact that this is a football club, then I was happy with good pitches."

The defender speaks about Carrington with a surprising degree of fondness for a player that entered the facility at its lowest point and now trains at the world-class City Football Academy [CFA].

"I keep it basic," he explains. "Start with good pitches, I'm happy. Fill it with good players, I'm even more happy. The rest is just bonus. It's extra."

Simon Pearce was about to go on a similar journey of discovery.

Commissioned by the incoming Chairman, Khaldoon Al Mubarak, to lead the due diligence process on behalf of ADUG, English-born Pearce was dispatched to the UK in the first week of September 2008 to get to know the Club and its key officials, identify its immediate needs, and lay the groundwork for Al Mubarak to come and complete the purchase on behalf of Sheikh Mansour.

Al Mubarak had first met Pearce – then a fly-in-fly-out consultant with international public relations firm, Burson-Marsteller – in 1998, when the two had worked together on an international gas pipeline project. He engineered Pearce's relocation to the Emirate on a full-time basis in 2006.

"My job was to triage the situation," says Pearce, of his first visit to Manchester City, "because I was not a publicly-known person, so it was easy for me to get off a plane and come and see everybody and find out where we were."

His first meeting was with Executive Chairman, Garry Cook, at the Club's commercial office on Park Lane, London, in a non-descript building across the street from the Hard Rock Café.

"I thought I was interviewing for the job of CEO," says Cook who, under the terms of his contract, could have walked away with three years' pay when the ownership changed hands. "At the end of the day, it is common knowledge that when somebody buys a football club they usually move in their own people, because it is a lot of money and they want it protected. So, we all just assumed we were interviewing. I did not realise it at the time, but he [Pearce] was the white knight on the horse."

"It was interesting," says Pearce, "because it was therapy for Garry. He was just explaining everything that was wrong with the Club."

"I prepared a small three-page document on what was going on," recalls Cook, "and I took a leap of faith really, because I basically gave him all of the dirty laundry."

The most pressing item on the agenda was the Club's parlous financial situation.

"In the weeks prior to this transaction, we were on the way to a complete and utter shutdown," says Cook. "We were heading for a massive catastrophe. I had alerted everybody from the Premier League, to Shinawatra himself, to whoever would listen really. It was really quite a drastic time. The Premier League knew what was going on."

The former Nike executive also shared with Pearce some of the more alarming things he had discovered since wading into the relatively murky world of football just four months earlier, including concerns related to irregular corporate governance and recruitment practices.

"I always used the analogy internally at the football club that it's like The Wizard of Oz," says Cook. "There is a yellow brick road that everybody thinks is the pathway to this utopia. Along the way though, you have got all these challenges and troubles and problems, and when you finally arrive at your destination, you pull back the curtain, and there is an old bloke with a microphone. This thing and this place was not what people thought it was, because the product we see on television is a media product, and behind all of that, with all of the cash transferring and money that is around, it just brings out the worst of the worst, and attracts some of the worst people."

Pearce, acutely aware of the invisible thread that now connected Manchester City and Abu Dhabi, was concerned by what he heard.

"So, when we started to get into all of this," recalls Cook, "his point to me was, 'We can't have this. I mean, really, we can't have this.' So, operation clean-up is really what it was."

It wasn't all therapy. Pearce and Cook also discussed a number of immediate business decisions that had to be made, including a potential new kit deal which was ultimately turned down.

Pearce then travelled to Manchester to meet with Vicky Kloss, then the Club's Head of Communications.

"Garry Cook phoned me and said there is a guy coming and he wants to meet. He is impressive, in his thirties," remembers a laughing Kloss. "It is all hush hush. No one needs to know."

The briefing was mysterious.

"I had to prepare some bullet points," remembers Kloss. "He wanted to understand what the communications team looked like, where we were strong, where were the gaps, and what were the myths out there that had already been created in the few days since the MOU."

With a communications background himself, it was a natural place for Pearce to start. However, coming so soon after the circus of deadline day, Kloss approached the meeting with scepticism.

"I wrote these two documents," she says. "One was the honest truth about the state of the Club and what had been going on, and the other was a polished version, because I didn't know the calibre or quality of this 'Simon' who, as far as I knew, was related to this guy that had been spouting stuff off day after day."

Kloss decided to play it by ear.

"I just thought I will go on a gut feel," she says. "If it is somebody that surprises me, and who seems decent and honest, then I will tell him the full truth, and I knew within 60 seconds of sitting down with Simon that I would."

The full truth was complicated, and gave Pearce actionable intelligence on some of the most powerful figures in and around the Club.

"The one thing I brought to that visit," says Pearce, "was that I said very little other than I apologised for the commentary about the deal from the Abu Dhabi side, and I said I was just there to listen. I wanted to learn as much as I possibly could, and I just let people speak for 48 hours."

Ten years later, Pearce and Kloss continue to have a close working relationship. Multiple people inside the Club say that their collaboration over the last ten years – combining Pearce's insights into the priorities of ADUG, and Kloss's innate understanding of the Mancunian perspective – has been integral to the project's success.

Jon Stemp, who has overseen a range of infrastructure projects at Manchester City since 2008, credits Kloss, a former detective with the Metropolitan Police and lifelong City supporter, with ensuring that the new owner and his representatives never forgot the historic importance of what they were taking on.

"Vicky was instrumental in getting the people coming into the leadership of the Club to understand that this thing had been there for 120 years," he says. "You've got something very important that you're in charge of now. Don't [expletive] it up. You're going to make changes, but understand what it is that you're changing."

On 5 September 2008, Pearce met with Cook, Mark Hughes [then first team Manager], Paul Aldridge [then COO], Jim Cassell [then Academy Director], Pairoj Piempongsant [a senior advisor to Thaksin Shinawatra] and Jack Srisumrid [an associate of Thaksin Shinawatra and then board member]. He was also given a tour of the Club's main facilities, including the City of Manchester Stadium, the Carrington training ground and the Academy at Platt Lane, all of which were leased.

At the end of that day, Pearce sent a preliminary update back to Al Mubarak and Sheikh Mansour in Abu Dhabi. Its conclusion was stark: "From these meetings it was ascertained that currently no business plan exists and no operations strategy is in place."

As newcomers to the Premier League, the undeveloped state of affairs came as a surprise to ADUG.

"What we imagined was going to be here was very different to what we found when we came here," says Al Mubarak. "I had, not a high expectation, but I had a minimum base case. I imagined there would be a minimum level of quality in terms of infrastructure, processes, systems and strategy. We came here and realised that we were way off. The infrastructure was horrendous. There was no strategy. There was no planning. There were no processes. There were no systems. You were literally building from scratch."

"Everything was broken," says Cook. "Training grounds, stadium, hospitality, offices. It was not one thing in particular. The whole place was broken and the organisation was not functioning properly."

Pearce recommended the commissioning of an outside management consultancy to conduct an initial assessment of the Club and support ADUG in the development of an interim business plan [a 5-week project known internally as Project Azure].

"We needed somebody to look at the business," says Pearce, "and help us identify the quick wins versus the medium-term wins, and ultimately, provide us with some advice on where the business needed to head."

The job went to Booz & Co. [now Strategy&], then recently spun off from Booz Allen Hamilton, which had advised on the wholesale restructuring of the Government of Abu Dhabi in 2005.

"The first thing we needed to do was just create a baseline," says Al Mubarak, "and that was what Simon worked on with Booz & Co. It was a management baseline of, what is the situation we have today, what's the assessment of what is available on the ground right now, and what needs to be done in the short to medium term, to really just get us up and running. That was step one. We hadn't even got to the long term."

The inadequacy of Carrington also caught Pearce's eye. Speculating that it was something Al Mubarak would want to fix right away, he commissioned a trusted contact in the sports and fitness industry [Stemp] to begin preparing plans to upgrade the facility shortly after the transaction was due to close.

Although he had uncovered a lot that needed to be done, Pearce says he came away from Manchester City with an overwhelming sense that the Club had immense potential that ADUG's backing could help unlock.

"The big take away for me was that there was goodwill at the Club," he says. "The people in there had that Mancunian spirit of, 'Well, we'll just give it a go.' There was a familiarity and a spirit of camaraderie that was clearly evident, and I knew we had the resources, so in my view, the foundation ingredients were present for this to succeed. I was very clear in my first report back to Khaldoon and His Highness that, actually, from an asset standpoint, we were not rich, but what you effectively had was permission to trade, because you were Manchester City, and you had unbelievable people, and you also had the supporter base."

On the basis of these findings, and the legal and financial due diligence that had taken place on a parallel track, Sheikh Mansour's ADUG was comfortable proceeding with the deal. Al Mubarak duly made plans to be in Manchester to complete the transaction and attend his first home game on 21 September 2008.

CHAPTER 3:

DIFFERENT DIRECTIONS

Historian Gary James hadn't seen Manchester City boss Garry Cook since the morning of 1 September, but a few weeks later he got a call from Cook's office asking him to come in on the weekend to give somebody a tour of the Stadium. James didn't ordinarily give tours, but was told that this one was important.

"I came in on this Saturday morning," says James. "I had no idea who I was supposed to be meeting, and I was sat in reception. Then Garry Cook, he came bouncing out again, right? He came up straight away and put his arm around me, 'Gaz, I am going to introduce you to Khaldoon Al Mubarak,' he said, 'He is going to be the Chairman. He wants to see the Stadium, and he wants to ask you some questions about the history of the Club. And tell him the truth. Don't lie. Don't try to say the Stadium is the best. Show him the crap.'"

"I thought, 'Well that's good,'" recalls James. "That's not normal for the owner or Chairman of a club to want to hear the truth. Quite often it's just, 'Tell us the good stuff.'"

Soon enough, James was face-to-face with Al Mubarak.

"So, I sit down with Khaldoon," says James, "and I'm good at judging people. I've always felt like I can sort of sense something in the first few minutes, and when I sat down I just knew that what Khaldoon was going to say was right. I just knew.

I just got this warm feeling, which I probably hadn't had with any other owner of City, ever."

James speaks from experience.

"I've interviewed every Chairman of City since '72," he says, "and the very first question Khaldoon asked me, not one of the other owners of the Club, or managing directors, or anybody, had ever asked, and that was, 'How, and why, does this football club exist? What happened?'"

The question caught him off guard.

"I thought, 'Right, this isn't some wealthy owner buying any football club and just thinking they can buy a few players and win the League. This is different.'"

Al Mubarak also enquired about some of the key figures in the Club's history, and James told him the story of Bert Trautmann, who would pass away five years later in July 2013.

"In my opinion, it is the sort of story that says what this Club is," he explains. "He was this German paratrooper, who won the Iron Cross for bravery, had escaped from the Russians, escaped from the Americans, was going to escape from the British and then thought, 'I won't bother anymore.' He became a hero at City after the war, and broke his neck in the Cup final [at Wembley in 1956]. It is such an incredible story, and it says so much about the fans' forgiveness, about bringing people in, about community, and all this sort of stuff."

James and Al Mubarak then embarked on an uncensored tour of the empty Stadium. The next day, Al Mubarak would return to the ground to attend his first home game alongside outgoing Chairman and former Thai Prime Minister, Thaksin Shinawatra, who would retain a 10% stake in Manchester City under the terms of the deal.

Al Mubarak was revealed as the incoming Chairman of Manchester City in an open letter from Sheikh Mansour that was published on the Club's website earlier that day. The letter confirmed that the sale would be completed two days later, gave Manager, Mark Hughes, the public backing of the new ownership, and made clear that no additional announcements would be made in the near future. It also put it in black and white that Sheikh Mansour was buying the Club in a private capacity.

It was in the Colin Bell Stand shortly before kick-off in that game against

Portsmouth FC on 21 September 2008 [which Manchester City won 6-0] that a beaming Shinawatra famously raised a visibly uncomfortable Al Mubarak's hand high in the air in an uncharacteristically triumphant greeting to the fans.

"You could see Khaldoon looked awkward," says Cook, who was standing just a few feet away when it happened. "He did not know it was coming. There's 50,000 people staring at you, one wants to tell the world, 'I am great, look at me, vote for me,' and the other one wants to say, 'I am just a guardian, I represent other people, and I don't want to bring shame or disrespect on them.' It was a clash of those two ideals. But, I do remember, after he did it, Khaldoon turned to me and said, 'Well, that was awkward.'"

Cook laughs.

"I always found him quite humorous, Khaldoon," he adds. "He has a good sense of humour."

"I'll never forget that game and that instance," says Al Mubarak, "because several things that were running through my mind that day I think were defining for the way I would treat my responsibility to this Club. The first thing is, there was such a positive energy. You could feel it in the whole Stadium. This was a true embrace of this new ownership, of Sheikh Mansour, and of me coming in as his Chairman. There was no scepticism, or cynicism, even though, to be fair, they had no idea who Sheikh Mansour was. They had no idea who I was. They had no idea if we were legit or not. But we got the complete benefit of the doubt. I felt it. We got the complete benefit of the doubt, day one. And that, to this day, remains something I hold dear, because they didn't have to do that, and this could have been very complicated and very difficult had it not been for the way that we were embraced."

Al Mubarak also began to form an idea of how he intended to approach the job of Chairman. And how he didn't.

"Just sitting next to Thaksin Shinawatra," he says, "and by the way, I have nothing negative to say about his way of doing it, but one thing I knew the second I sat there for the first time is, I am not that in any way, shape or form. I'm not a politician. We couldn't have been further apart in the way I saw the role, and the way he did. Not that I would say there is anything wrong with his way. It's just, the one thing I knew is, I'm not that, and I knew that the second I sat down for that first game. I knew, that's not what I'm going to be doing. It's not going to be like this."

That led the new Chairman to another unavoidable conclusion.

"I also knew, at that moment really, that the [90/10] partnership was not going to work, and that we needed to get into full ownership as soon as possible. There were just two approaches that were going in completely different directions. And I think, for this to be successful, I knew at that moment, we just needed to exit that, and have full control."

Sheikh Mansour's ADUG would own 100 per cent of Manchester City exactly one year later on 21 September 2009.

"It was a smooth detachment," says Al Mubarak of the eventual buyout, "but it was clear. We were going in different directions."

CHAPTER 4:

HIT THE GROUND RUNNING FOR YOUR LIFE

Marty Edelman was having dinner with Sheikh Mansour bin Zayed Al Nahyan and his brother, Sheikh Tahnoon, just hours after the world had learned that ADUG was in the process of buying Manchester City.

A respected New York City attorney, Edelman had worked on a series of projects in Abu Dhabi since 2002, was extremely well-connected there, and at that time was directly involved in the establishment of New York University Abu Dhabi, which would officially open its doors in 2010.

"Sheikh Mansour said, 'You know a lot about football,'" recalls Edelman. "And I said, 'Well, I know a lot about American football,' because the year before I had represented Steve Ross [CEO and Founder of Related Companies] in buying the Miami Dolphins."

The distinction was brushed aside.

"He said, 'Khaldoon [Al Mubarak] is going to form a board, and I want you to work with him,' says Edelman. "I said, 'Okay, I think it would be great,' and then Khaldoon called me the next day."

It didn't take long for Edelman's limited background in English football to reveal itself.

"The first meeting I came to here in Manchester," he recalls, "we were sitting around the table and everybody was talking about relegation. I leaned over to Simon Pearce and said, 'What the [expletive] is relegation?'"

Pearce couldn't keep it to himself.

"Of course, he burst out laughing," says Edelman, "and then the whole room had to know what he was laughing about, so naturally he told them, and I was sitting there probably turning eight shades of a colour."

Relegation would soon be less of a laughing matter around the boardroom table at Manchester City. By Christmas Day 2008, the team had dropped to 18th in the table and found itself squarely in the relegation zone. While the ink was still drying on the contracts of sale, Manchester City was at risk of falling out of the Premier League.

"Can you imagine?" says Al Mubarak. "We got in there in September. By December we were fighting relegation, and I was like, 'What are we dealing with here?'. I mean, okay, it didn't turn out that way, and we made some emergency investments in January [2009] to buy in a couple of players [Bellamy, Bridge, de Jong, Given, along with a failed bid for Kaká], but it was a stressful year, because I could have never anticipated, even that September, that it was going to be this hard. And not only that it was going to be hard, but that we could have faced annihilation and collapse because we could have been relegated, and imagine then what we would have had to deal with!"

It is hard to imagine Manchester City on the brink of relegation today.

"That first year [2008-09]," says Pearce, "our ambition was to get to 40 points to prevent relegation. That was it. This season [2017-18], we set the record for the fastest club to 40 points in the history of the League."

According to Al Mubarak, the new ownership spent most of that first year in survival mode.

"Really, that first 12 months was patchwork and emergency surgery just to keep things together," he says. "I wouldn't say it counts in the long-term vision, because the first year was just baselining and fixing and trying to get ourselves up and running. It was really that next summer [2009], which was the first real summer of preparation, when we started putting together a long-term strategy, a long-term vision for the Club, and we started to get a hold of the finances and the human capital side of it. That work, the real journey, started for me in the summer of 2009."

One of the first pieces of patchwork to be approved after the takeover was an immediate upgrade to the Carrington gym.

"I was in Biarritz on my honeymoon when I got a phone call from Simon [Pearce] saying, 'We need you to be in Manchester on Monday. We just bought a football club,'" recalls Jon Stemp. "I said to him, 'What colour is it?', and he said, "It's the blue one," and so I said 'Sure.'"

Stemp arrived in Manchester a few days later with a loose brief and a tight timeline.

"Khaldoon and Simon felt that the improvement of the training facility was an easy fix," he says. "It was visual, it was material, and it would help the team. I think we had 4 or 5 weeks to plan it and build it, because we wanted to build it while the international break was on, when the players would be away for 10 days, and then they would come back and things would different."

The old gym at Carrington wasn't exactly a renovator's dream.

"It was an old sports and social club that had belonged to Shell Chemicals," says Pete Bradshaw, Director of Infrastructure & Estates at Manchester City, who had been at the Club since 2003 and worked with Stemp on the gym upgrade. "It had previously been used by a university and subsequently by ourselves. The place had been knocked about and it was never really fit for purpose. In the short term we had to make it fit for purpose and therefore we had to expand the gym, bringing it up to date."

According to Stemp, the way that the project was executed was as important as the outcome.

"It was important that the project wasn't done to the workforce," he explains. "These were good sport scientists, good doctors, good trainers, good facilities management people, and they'd had to do without the right things for the longest time, so we started a process of talking to people to say, 'Well, we're going to improve it. What do you need?'"

Some of the responses were startlingly modest.

"They would sort of answer by saying, 'Well, I need a new bucket,'" recalls Stemp, "which of course they did, but when I said, 'Well, why do you need a new bucket?', they'd say, 'Because the cleaning store is on the other side of the building.' So, then I'd say, 'Well, if we move the cleaning store, would that help you?', and they'd say 'Oh yes, that would save me half my working day, because I could stop walking from one end of the building to the other!'"

Bradshaw says these initial reactions were understandable at the time.

"What you have got to remember is that we had gone through quite a few years of seriously watching the pennies, and people bringing things from home to get the work done," he says. "We had gone through periods where it was challenging to pay the staff. We could not order stationery. We would bring pens and pencils from home for a while. There were hard times and the staff that went through that, that is what they got used to. It made them prudent as well. They had to think about what they were buying. They had to justify why they needed a piece of kit, so to some people, a lawn mower or some stationery or a set of goals was priceless, and practically it was what they needed. If you then come along and say the day after, 'Look, the world is your oyster, what do you want?', it can be quite challenging for people."

Stemp maintains it was an important exercise that set a new tone for what was to come.

"We were able to execute it with the participation of the staff," he says, "so when it opened, everybody who worked there had some ownership of the new gym that they had helped make happen. So, it wasn't just the gym, it was a process of galvanising a workforce to a new ownership who were going to help them, and give them the tools to be better at what they did."

The players returned to a whole new environment.

"We came back and they'd done one of those things you'd see on 'Extreme Makeovers' or something," recalls Vincent Kompany. "They'd changed the whole entire training facility. It was all short term, makeshift, but it looked a million dollars, and it was literally two weeks, which was incredible."

"Physical change is a very powerful statement of intent," said Stemp privately back in 2010. "You can have words, but unless you see physical change it doesn't become real. So, when the players came back from international duty and they walked into this mezzanined gym with 80 fitness stations and all the latest pre-activation areas, designed how the sports coaches wanted it, with all the latest toys, they were just like, 'Oh, so this is it. This is what the future's about.'"

Pearce insists that the gym upgrade was functionally necessary, but agrees that at least partially, it was also an exercise in internal communications.

"We needed to change the gym to send a message that the culture needs to change," he says, "and that this is not the organisation that it was yesterday. It wasn't the best gym in the world, but it was an exceptional use of that space."

It was also one of the earliest manifestations of an organisation-wide rebuilding process that ramped up across the Club at that time. The breadth of the transformation that occurred during this period [the first phase of a three-phase "Fix, Build and Grow" strategy championed internally by Cook with his trademark fervour] should not be underestimated.

In 2009, the majority of the Club's employees moved out of the City of Manchester Stadium into a newly-constructed office building [City@Home] with its own Starbucks on the ground floor. That same year, the Club built a new box office that meant people would no longer have to queue up in the rain or snow to buy tickets. In 2010, a range of employee benefits were introduced at the Club for the first time, including private medical and life insurance for all eligible staff. The organisation also grew rapidly in size, as Manchester City hired more than 140 new employees in the first two years after the ADUG takeover.

"All of that was about expanding our ability to be better," says Cook. "To be one of the world's best, you have got to be better than you are, and we basically just said, 'Mediocrity is unacceptable, and everybody here has to get better.' So, we cleaned up everything, we introduced new systems, we introduced new accounting procedures, we introduced board reports, we introduced all-staff meetings. We just went through the whole thing, soup to nuts. My argument at the time was that the football on the pitch will be the manifestation of everything else. It will all bleed into being better, and then you can get to a point where you actually say to players, 'If you want to come here and be proud, then come here and play for us. If you are not that bothered by it, then you need to go somewhere else, because everybody else here cares.'"

"If you look at the transformation that the Club has undergone over the last 12 months, it's across the board," Al Mubarak told CityTV in 2009, citing a raft of recent improvements to the Club's physical infrastructure and organisational capabilities. "It's a new City, but it's a new City that has retained its soul, and evolved."

Bradshaw maintains that at the time of the takeover, there was already an awareness within the Club that things needed to change, but acknowledges the arrival of ADUG transformed the boundaries of what could be accomplished.

"We could do things better than we had done in the past," he says, "and bring some new outside thinking into this, and that changed the way we did lots of things. We moved to a different level, a much, much better level. More efficient. More visionary, I suppose, where we could actually see a future plan. The one thing we had been in the past was reactive. Now we were being very forward looking, and we could plan things in a far better way. I think that is what changed more than anything else."

CHAPTER 5:

CHANGE MANAGEMENT

A key recommendation of the Project Azure analysis produced by Booz & Co. [now Strategy&] shortly after the ADUG takeover was the appointment of an individual, separate to the first team Manager, with overarching responsibility for all aspects of the Club's sprawling football operations. At many European clubs, that person was known as the Football Director. At Manchester City, the position was branded the Chief Football Administration Officer, largely for political reasons.

"People forget that back then there was a negative association with the Football Director job in England," says Manchester City Chairman, Khaldoon Al Mubarak. "This was an era where you had the Alex Fergusons of the world, where you had the Arsène Wengers of the world, who were heralded as great successes because they had full control over the running of the football teams and the organisations across the board. Now it is the norm, but back then there was a negative connotation that came with the role, so we had to do it carefully. We had to do it one step at a time."

The first step was finding a candidate, and Garry Cook [retained by the new ownership as CEO of Manchester City] had his sights set firmly on the former Sheffield Wednesday and Arsenal winger, Brian Marwood, with whom he had worked at Nike, where Marwood was UK Football Sports Marketing Manager.

"I needed somebody who thought commercially, and not just about football, free kicks and corners," says Cook. "He had played at the highest level so he was respected by his profession. He had also been in those Nike corporate meetings, and had been around the corporate world, and at that time, I was trying to extoll the virtues of Nike into our business. Brian had been through all of that, and he had relationships with players and agents because he was signing boot deals with a lot of them. He knew the football world."

In fact, Cook had already tried at least once to convince Marwood to join him at Manchester City.

"Garry initially asked me before the new owners came in," says Marwood. "We were colleagues at Nike together, and we'd had many conversations about football, and he just called me out of the blue one day, and we chewed the fat a little bit, and then he said, 'I want somebody that knows football here, and I'd like you to consider coming.' I said, 'Okay, I am interested,' and I really could see myself working with Garry. I really like Garry. But I said 'I need to meet the people involved,' and he set up a meeting in London for me to meet some of the owners, and it just didn't feel right."

Marwood struggles to put his finger on what turned him off.

"Don't ask me what it was," he says. "It just didn't feel right, and to give up the stability of what I had for that, I just didn't get a good feeling about it. I had a good job at Nike. I was co-commentating for Sky Television. So, you know, life was fine. I said to Garry, 'It's just not for me.'"

After the Club changed hands in September 2008, a persistent Cook tried again, and Marwood agreed to sit down with the new Chairman over lunch at the Halkin hotel in London.

Riding the train down from Durham to Kings Cross that morning, Marwood was unsure what to expect.

"Obviously, I didn't know Khaldoon," he says, recalling that first encounter. "My perception probably wasn't in a good place, because I'd had the previous discussion, and then there had been the takeover, Robinho, and the Kaká thing. It just seemed to be a bit of a laughing stock. I mean, I couldn't have been further from the truth, but that was my perception travelling down on the train. I was probably intrigued more than anything else."

What was scheduled as a 90-minute lunch became a four-hour discussion about football and the future of Manchester City.

"It's easy to say now," says Marwood, "but I can honestly tell you that I trusted him 100 per cent from that meeting. I could sense that passion. I could sense he was a person that really wanted to take this football club forward. It was just something that I walked away from going, 'Yeah, this feels right.'"

Al Mubarak recalls coming away from the meeting with an equally positive feeling.

"I was very impressed with Brian," he says. "There are very few people in the world that when you meet them for the first time, you know, this man has integrity. And with Marwood I knew it at that first meeting. And for me, by the way, that was a condition precedent for anyone I was going to hire for that job, because, in that job, if you get someone with questionable integrity… I mean, you could get taken to the cleaners."

Marwood also passed the Chairman's sycophancy test.

"He is a straight shooter," says Al Mubarak. "I asked him questions that were purposely leading him to be critical of what we were doing, and he didn't shy away, and I think that gave me a lot of confidence. I left that meeting and I didn't need another session."

Marwood joined Manchester City in March 2009 with a diplomatic title but a broad mandate.

"We wanted to bring a best-in-class environment to key areas such as scouting and recruitment, coaching, medical, sports science, player welfare and performance analysis," he explains. "They were the six big core areas. I had to look at all of those areas individually, look at the people, and look at where they were at in terms of, 'Were they best-in-class or where did they rank?'"

He would also work closely with then Manager Mark Hughes, Cook and Al Mubarak, among others, to assemble a first team squad capable of meeting the Club's growing ambitions.

Manchester City made its biggest moves yet in the summer of 2009, signing Carlos Tevez, Kolo Touré, Stuart Taylor, Roque Santa Cruz, Emmanuel Adebayor, Sylvinho, Gareth Barry and Joleon Lescott in quick succession.

Not everybody welcomed the aggressive approach.

"I remember one of the first signings," says Marwood. "It might have been the first signing I made. Gareth Barry was coming, and he was with the England squad, and we had to take him for a medical at Bushey, near Watford, because the England squad were staying around there at the time. I remember picking him up and we were in the car going to Bushey, and [UK-based sports radio station] talkSPORT was on, and the story had broken that we were signing Gareth Barry."

As Marwood remembers it, the commentariat wasn't applauding the move.

"Gareth is a super pro and a super person," he says, "and they were absolutely caning him, saying things like, 'He won't win anything at Man City, he's only going there for the money, plastic club, seen all this before, foreign owners coming in, killing the game, these guys are mercenaries.' That was the narrative, and I said to him, 'Do you want me to turn this off?' and he went 'No, I want to listen to it,' and I said 'Yeah, but they're not saying particularly nice things about you, or the Club, or any of it.' He said 'I'm not bothered. I'm just going to remember this, because I want to show these people they are wrong.' That's when you know you're getting the right people, and people like Gareth were so important to where we are now."

Barry says the intense reaction didn't surprise him.

"I realised at the time it was going to be a big move at a stage where you're coming into your prime – your peak years – so it was something I had to think about really deep because there were a couple [of options]," he says. "Liverpool were still interested in me, Arsenal were asking a few questions about my situation, and obviously I had the chance to sign a new long-term contract at Villa and stay there and possibly be a one club man. But the signs I was getting from Manchester City, and the conversations I had with Brian Marwood, were really positive and really ambitious."

"It was so easy for everyone else just to kill him for it being about money," says Vicky Kloss, who recalls homegrown players such as Barry and Joleon Lescott getting hit particularly hard for joining Manchester City at the time. "Those two stick with me because they were derided as mercenaries when, the reality was, they were anything but that. They were talented and ambitious professionals who were good human beings too. They were really central to our achievements in the years which were to follow."

Lescott says that at least for him, the move was less about money than it was about the chance to enjoy success in the peak years of his career.

"18 months before I had signed a new contract at Everton, and that had secured my future anyway," he says. "I was 27, so in terms of my prime, I had five years left. So, I was thinking, in the next five years, who is going to win more? When someone is trying to get to the top they're not going to come back next year, when you're 28. I didn't want them to get someone else. I wanted it to be me."

Although it's doubtful that either player would have taken a pay cut to join Manchester City, Barry agrees that the chance to bring silverware to a club that hadn't won anything in a long time was a factor in his decision.

"When I spoke to Mark Hughes he mentioned as well that the Club hadn't won a trophy for a while," says Barry, "and for me that was a big pull to try and be a part of the team that was able to eventually get City over the line and win a trophy."

The Club's recent activity in the transfer market suggested it would only be a matter of time.

"Of course, I looked at who they'd signed," says Lescott. "Tevez, Adebayor, Kolo Touré, Barry, de Jong, Robinho. You're not going to finish midtable with Carlos Tevez, even if he played on his own."

Even so, Barry credits the Manchester City fan base for keeping their expectations in check during this period.

"The fans were aware that there was a lot of money spent," says Barry, "and they could've easily expected it straight away, but I got the sense that they were willing to be patient. It's easy to get carried away, but I didn't feel like they put too much pressure on the players. Obviously at times they can get frustrated, but my general feeling was they were really patient and they deserved the trophies in the end."

Lescott agrees.

"Expectations didn't change," he says. "I never felt from the fans that we had to win. That never happened at City. There was never a time when we were losing and the fans booed us off. They never forgot the previous 40 years. Soon, that might be forgotten."

The fans may have been prepared to wait, but by mid-December 2009, the key decision-makers at Manchester City had run out of patience with Manager Mark Hughes, and resolved to replace him with former Inter Milan boss, Roberto Mancini, before Christmas.

"I think Mark Hughes would've eventually got it right," says Barry. "As you know in football, you don't get that chance. We started really well. I think we won the first three or four games on the spin, but we had a run of games where we kept drawing. We couldn't see games out, and kept conceding late, and those wins weren't happening and were turning into draws, [and] eventually they called time."

History suggests it was the right call, but in what journalist David Conn described in his 2012 book, 'Richer Than God,' as "the most miserable mishap of the Abu Dhabi reign at Manchester City," the carefully choreographed transition from Hughes to Mancini blew up in the face of everybody involved.[3]

The plan was for Hughes to be given the bad news behind closed doors after the team played Sunderland on 19 December 2009. However, when Mancini's imminent appointment leaked earlier that day, Hughes was in the unenviable position of having to go out and coach his final game as a lame duck. The Club could have scrambled and brought the announcement forward, but that would have meant abruptly sacking Hughes in the lead-up to the game, and before the Chairman could meet with him face-to-face.

"The intention, of course, was to tell Mark immediately after the game on Saturday," explained Garry Cook, at a tense press conference three days later. "Regrettably, and I repeat, regrettably, against all of our efforts, the rumours of discussions with Roberto Mancini became public before the game. Once Mark was informed, I informed his staff, and then consequently, the players themselves were informed."

City officials acknowledge it was an unedifying episode.

"The day it all unfolded was probably one of the worst days of my tenure here," says Marwood. "You had this game against Sunderland that I think we ended up winning 4-3, which was a bizarre game and could have ended up 10-10, but everybody in the crowd knew that Mark was leaving. And irrespective of whether Mark was the right guy or the wrong guy for us, you would never want anybody to go through that."

"It was absolutely disrespectful to Mark, and absolutely disrespectful to his team," acknowledges Cook, looking back on these events today. "It put a dent in the football club, and if I had the time again, I would have done it differently. But, what I also realised, and one of the most valuable lessons from it all, was that it does not matter who you are in a football club, whether you are a board member, an owner, an agent, a player, a manager, or a representative, somebody is always going to do something that you do not know about."

The awkward nature of Hughes's departure wasn't ideal for the new boss either. In his 2012 book about Mancini, Stuart Brennan of the Manchester Evening News described the uphill battle faced by the incoming Manager.

"City fans were largely happy with the fact that Hughes had gone," he wrote, "but embarrassed by the cack-handed way in which the transition had occurred, and they were unsure about Mancini's pedigree... [He] had to earn the respect of the fans and of his players, and the only way to do that would be by winning matches and showing signs of real progress."[4]

Mancini would do that in style.

CHAPTER 6:

MANCINI

Roberto Mancini's debut as Manager of Manchester City was at home against Stoke City on 26 December 2009. The Club's Head of Communications, Vicky Kloss, met with him shortly before kick-off in an office adjacent to the pitch-side tunnel. It's always cold on Boxing Day, and on this particular afternoon, Kloss wore an old blue and white scarf that the Club had given away free to its fans after an underwhelming season in 2002-03.

"I had met him a couple of times by then," says Kloss. "I had done his first press conference and I would have also done a pre-match press conference with him, but this was talking him through how he was going to be introduced to the crowd."

Mancini came to Manchester with strong credentials. The winner of an array of Italian and European trophies as a player [including two Serie A titles, seven Coppa Italia titles, two Supercoppa Italiana titles, and two UEFA Cup Winners' Cups], he had then transitioned seamlessly into a career in management, winning Coppa Italia titles at both Fiorentina and Lazio, before moving to Inter Milan in 2004 where he delivered two Coppa Italia titles, two Supercoppa Italiana titles, and three consecutive Serie A titles in just four years.

However, with the fallout ongoing from the public humiliation of Hughes, there was still some uncertainty over the reception that awaited his replacement.

"I said 'You know, anything that you can do, Roberto, to align yourself with our fans or to connect with them very early on, would be helpful,'" says Kloss. "'If they sing your name, it's a good thing to acknowledge. You know all this anyway, because you've done it before, but anything you can do [would be welcome].'"

Mancini's eyes fell on the freebie scarf.

"He sort of looks at me, and he looks at my scarf," recalls Kloss, "and I said, 'You can have it if you like, because I know you like a scarf, and you wearing that? They would love you for it.' It was like a little injection of panache in the Northwest of England."

As it turned out, the fans were set to give Mancini a broadly supportive welcome anyway, and the team produced a convincing 2-0 win in his first game in charge.

"The crowd loved him," recalls former CEO Garry Cook, of Mancini's immediate chemistry with the City faithful. "The audience loved everything about him, and that scarf became world famous."

With his first win under his belt, the new boss wasted no time in putting his own stamp on the team, beginning with an increased emphasis on defence.

"Mancini was a completely different type of manager," says Vincent Kompany. "Very hands on. Very Italian in many ways. But you know, what Mancini gave us, and me, is that we had an incredibly solid defensive block when he was there. That was almost the priority for the team at the time, and that was the key thing with Mancini. And I think that remains as well. I got so many defensive principles from what he brought from his country, and anything I've learned I've passed on to defenders and players around me as well, so it still kind of lives within the team."

"When Mancini came in, it was very different," says Joleon Lescott. "It was very rigid. [Fabio] Capello was the England Manager then so I was used to a similar regime. Mancini was very thorough, but it was probably what we needed. When you've got Carlos [Tevez], Bellers [Craig Bellamy] and the various attacking threats, you're going to score. He brought the discipline at both ends of the pitch."

"Mancini was a completely different character [to Hughes]," says Gareth Barry, who agrees that playing under Capello for England was good preparation for Mancini. "Even training times. He liked to train at night sometimes, so you'd be there at the training ground and we didn't really have enough light from the floodlights at that time, but he was adamant that that's the time we train, so you've got to work with it. I can't even remember what we used, portable floodlights or a car light shining on the pitch, but yeah, he was very big on discipline. His training methods were completely different to what players were used to. Some players didn't like it, others just got on with it, but ultimately it's all about results and he found a way to win games."

Mancini won his first four games in a row as Manager of Manchester City. Speaking to the media in January 2010, he sought to rein in the rising expectations around the Club.

"I am not a magician, I am a manager," he said. "Hard work will improve us and that is the aim this season, to improve game on game and see where we end up in the League and the Cups."

Earlier that month, Mancini had made Patrick Vieira his first signing at Manchester City, citing the veteran midfielder's winning mentality, Premier League experience, and familiarity with the Manager and his staff from their time together at Inter Milan as key factors in the decision.

Vieira is refreshingly honest about what was on his mind at the time.

"I joined City because I wanted to be part of the French national team for the World Cup in 2010," he says. "I was playing for Inter Milan, and [Jose] Mourinho was the coach at the time, and I was not playing a lot. I needed to play every week. So, it was an important deal for me to go to City, and play with the coach that I used to have, and that was supposed to help me to get to the French national team for the World Cup."

Sources with knowledge of the situation say the Vieira deal almost collapsed when the then 33-year-old initially failed his medical, but Mancini, Cook, Brian Marwood, and ultimately, the Chairman, Khaldoon Al Mubarak, agreed to proceed with his signing anyway on the basis of what they believed he would bring to the Club.

Vieira didn't end up making the 2010 World Cup, but his relationship with Manchester City would evolve over the next eight years in ways that nobody, himself included, could possibly have predicted when he signed that original six-month deal.

Apart from the addition of Vieira, and the loaning out of a number of players [including Robinho], the new Manager closed out the 2009-10 season with a squad largely inherited from his predecessor. Under Mancini, that side came close to a top four finish [and qualification for the UEFA Champions League], but ended up fifth after losing 1-0 at home to Tottenham [who claimed fourth spot by three points] in the second-last game of the season.

Despite missing out on a place in the UEFA Champions League, after less than a year in the job, Mancini made clear that his ambitions for Manchester City were already greater than a top four finish.

'It's not my mentality to play for fourth position," he told the Daily Mail's Mark Ryan in 2010 while on pre-season tour in the United States. "I don't think like this. I am very optimistic. This [2010-11] is going to be a good season for us. If the players follow me and trust me, if we all work really hard, we can change the history of this club."[5]

In advance of the 2010-11 season, the squad was strengthened with a number of new recruits, including Jerome Boateng, David Silva, Yaya Touré, Mario Balotelli, Aleksandar Kolarov and James Milner. Mancini also had goalkeeper Joe Hart recalled from Birmingham City where he had spent the previous season on loan. The mix of new signings, and the Manager's plans for each of them, suggested there would be more to the Mancini era than a solid defence.

"In Barcelona, I was playing deeper," explains Yaya Touré, "but Mancini really knew me. When I came to City, at the beginning it was quite difficult. I needed adaptation. But I remember, I was sitting in his office, we were talking together, and he was saying, 'You can play forward.' I said 'No, me, I like to touch the ball, I want to be a midfielder.' He said, 'No, no, no, I want you to stay in front, because I know when you get the ball, you can go forward. You can do anything you want.'"

Mancini didn't deploy Yaya Touré as a forward, but the midfielder says the conversation had a lasting impact on his confidence.

"I think Mancini was a big, big, big mentor," he says. "He was working on my head, as well. He was trying to improve me. He's the guy who gave me trust in myself, and belief. Because when you have a manager who believes in you, and says that you can do what you want, like he believed in me, it's big. For me, the more trust people have in me, the more I can give it to them. I was very happy to work with Mancini. This guy, he helped me a lot."

Not everybody that worked with Mancini found him to be quite as helpful. Although City officials are careful not to openly criticise their former Manager on the record, it is widely known that Mancini's combative personality did put a few noses out of joint during his time at the Club. The fractious nature of his relationship with Chief Football Administration Officer, Brian Marwood, for example, spilled into public view on more than one occasion.

Although they had a difficult working relationship, Marwood doesn't dispute that Mancini produced results at a club that had not won anything in more than three decades.

"I will always say that as much as it didn't work out between us, he really played a huge part in creating best-in-class standards," he says. "He was very demanding on everybody, and he brought in a set of demands when he came into the Club that upset people, made people uncomfortable, but gave people that drive to prove him wrong."

"Roberto is not an easy character," admits Manchester City Chairman, Khaldoon Al Mubarak, who hand-picked Mancini and had a better relationship with him than most. "He's definitely very demanding. He's got a strong personality that, you know, has its pros and has its cons."

Mancini developed a very close relationship with the Chairman, with the two in daily contact by phone at various points. Al Mubarak, who stresses he is generally hesitant to circumvent the Club's chain of command, believes the Chairman-Manager nexus is a special case.

"I think, in any football organisation, the relationship between the Chairman and the Manager is crucial," he says. "That relationship has to be on the same wave length. There is a personal trust that needs to be built for success to come. And it's not easy because its personality driven, but it's necessary. You can't have mistrust, I think, between the Chairman and the Manager. There's always going to be friction in many places within the organisation, between the Football Director and the Manager, between the Manager and the CEO. That happens in this business, and sometimes that friction is healthy, sometimes it is not. It depends on the personalities involved. But I think the relationship between the Chairman and the Manager is such a crucial one that you cannot have that friction, and you cannot have that misalignment."

Mancini left no doubt over where he saw himself in the Club's hierarchy, telling The

Guardian's Daniel Taylor in 2013, "Above me there is only Khaldoon [Al Mubarak] and Sheikh Mansour."[6]

Although the Manager's direct line to the Chairman would lead to certain issues landing on Al Mubarak's desk in Abu Dhabi that probably didn't belong there, Mancini's coaching ability and football IQ were undeniable. In the second half of the 2009-10 season, his first four-and-a-half months in charge, Manchester City won 11 out of 21 games in the Premier League [losing 5 and drawing 5], and memorably beat Manchester United in the first leg of the semi-finals of the League Cup in January 2010, before falling short in the second leg.

It was a promising start and, despite the hit they had taken over their treatment of Hughes, Manchester City and ADUG officials were confident that they had made the right decision.

"His personality could be difficult to manage," says Cook, "but I loved him because he won football matches, and that was what we needed."

At the end of the 2009-10 season, Roberto Mancini gave Vicky Kloss an unexpected gift. Hidden beneath the packaging was a delicate blue and white scarf.

"I don't know if others got the same thing," she says. "I didn't see anybody that did, so maybe it was him remembering that I had given him mine. He never expressly said that, but either way it was a nice thing to do. Actually, it was a very nice touch."

CHAPTER 7:

FROM PRICE TAKERS TO PLACE MAKERS

Manchester City signed more than 20 first team players between 2009 and 2011.

"It was a whirlwind," says Brian Marwood, then Manchester City's Chief Football Administration Officer. "We were on planes all the time, we were on the phone all the time, we were in cars all the time, we were working things out. We were doing late nights in the office and early morning starts, and going through the pain of losing a player and then the joy of getting one, and dealing with all of these different situations. At times it felt a bit seat of the pants, but we got stuff done."

Those close to the process say that for every player that was eventually signed, the Club's football department would have done the same amount of homework on around four or five alternatives.

"It is very rare that you have something that is just smooth and uncomplicated," says Marwood. "You might be going for one target and that one falls through, so you need another one. You've got to keep a number of plates spinning."

Derided by many as 'buying success,' the ADUG strategy was unashamedly based on the theory that investing in world-class players was the fastest and most reliable way for Manchester City to become more competitive on the pitch, which the new ownership believed was a prerequisite for everything else that it intended to do.

"A successful team on the pitch makes everything simpler," explains John MacBeath, who was appointed to the Manchester City board in 2010, and would serve as interim CEO from September 2011 to August 2012. "You can sell your tickets for your games a lot easier. More people want to come. In the modern era, more people want to watch it on television internationally, therefore more sponsors are potentially interested in you. And once you've got that inflow of capital, the cash that comes from being successful on the pitch, it opens up a whole panorama of additional opportunities to you, because then you can make choices."

"Our strategy was to accelerate," confirmed then CEO Garry Cook speaking privately in 2010. "Our strategy was to take five years of financial resources and invest them in the football team to get us to Champions League standard. Now we've accelerated and we've done it all in two years."

"I always liken it to putting the roof on before we built any walls and put any foundations in," says Marwood, of the Club's accelerated recruitment strategy. "Actually, it was the right thing to do, because at that stage we were only just becoming aware of the impact that Financial Fair Play was going to have on our business."

Financial Fair Play [FFP] was a controversial set of regulations approved in 2010 [phased in from 2011-12 onwards] that required clubs competing in major European competitions – such as the UEFA Champions League and UEFA Europa League – to be able to demonstrate to UEFA that they were breaking even. According to UEFA, the system was designed to improve the overall financial sustainability of European club football, and included a range of sanctions for clubs that failed to comply. The advent of FFP posed an immediate challenge to ADUG's long-term strategy for Manchester City, which was to invest heavily in the early years in order to quickly become competitive, without necessarily breaking even on an annual basis.

As the Club and its ambitious owner raced to beat the closing door, not every move worked out as well as they had hoped.

"We were building a side very quickly," says Marwood, "so sometimes you would break your own rules. Roque Santa Cruz [2009] was a great example. He was always top of Mark's list, but we knew his availability wasn't great [due to injuries], and this was potentially an £18 million transfer, so it wasn't an insignificant amount of money. We brought him in, but we had a question mark, and unfortunately, he didn't play as many times as we would have liked because he had some recurring injuries, but he was a great person."

Some possessed raw talent that made them a risk worth taking.

"You know when Mario [Balotelli] came [2010], we knew all about Mario, so there were no surprises," says Marwood. "The important thing was to put the welfare piece around him, but Roberto was so keen on getting him. He had given Mario his debut at Inter Milan and he knew what he was capable of doing, but he also knew what Mario was about. Mario was probably just the modern-day Paul Gascoigne. He wasn't malicious and nasty, he just used to do some daft silly things."

"Balotelli I have known since I gave him his debut at 17," Mancini told the Daily Mail's Martin Samuel in 2010. "Outside the pitch, he does things and it might be better he did not — but he is 20. I do not know too many perfect 20-year-olds. I was never perfect when I played, either. Good players are not perfect."[7]

Two years later, Mancini and Balotelli would be photographed having a physical altercation at the Club's Carrington training ground, where they reportedly had to be separated by other members of the coaching staff. It didn't look like a big deal in the photos, but it wasn't a great sight either.

Other signings from that period, including David Silva [2010], Yaya Touré [2010] and Sergio Agüero [2011], plus Vincent Kompany [signed in 2008 and retained on a new 5-year deal in 2009], would become long-term fixtures that would still be winning trophies for Manchester City in 2018. Patrick Vieira [2009] would join Manchester City's executive team at the end of his playing career in 2011, before coaching the Club's Elite Development Squad on his way to being appointed Head Coach of New York City FC in 2015.

To begin with, Manchester City had to pay a premium to attract players of the calibre it wanted.

"We spent more money than others," admits Marwood, "but I had seen this in my previous life with Nike, because when Nike was trying to get into football, Nike had to overpay, but once they got in and people saw they were a credible brand producing great product and having success, actually the numbers came down rather than went up."

To say that Manchester City spent a lot between 2009 and 2011 is an understatement. The balance sheet was a bloodbath. In 2009-10, the Club reported an annual loss of £121.3m. In 2010-11, it reported an annual loss of £197.4m, the largest ever recorded in English football. The most positive spin that could be put on it in the Club's Annual Report that year was that it represented the "bottoming out" of losses before things could be expected to turn around.

The critics weren't backward in coming forward. In 2009, Arsenal Manager Arsène Wenger accused the Club of "financial doping." In 2010, Manchester United Manager Sir Alex Ferguson took a veiled swipe at "kamikaze spending" in the game. In 2011, Karl-Heinz Rummenigge, the Chairman of Bayern Munich, made a pre-emptive call for Manchester City to be excluded from international and European competitions on the basis of its financial performance. Perhaps topping them all, The Mirror reported on one of Manchester City's most important signings of the decade with the immortal headline: "How Barca reserve Yaya Touré was seduced by the whore of world football."[8]

Manchester City board member Simon Pearce bristles at any perceived criticism of the Club's financial management during this period.

"Let's be clear about what we were doing," he says. "The very premise of your question is 'You were losing loads of money.' No, we were investing aggressively in order to produce a return. We wouldn't have needed to invest that aggressively if the regulators hadn't been creating a closed shop for the existing status quo within the world of football. You effectively had a complete, protected regulatory environment for those that had already achieved a place within the upper echelons of the football hierarchy, and what we were fighting against was protectionism."

"You had immense pressure coming in from markets such as Italy, Spain and Germany against what we were doing," agrees Chairman, Khaldoon Al Mubarak, "and that's when FFP was coming up, and they were going after us, right, left and front. It was clear at that point that, in that environment, the system was not going to swallow us easily, and was not going to accept what we were doing, so it was important for us to find interesting ways to grow our business within the constraints of the environment we were living in."

"Whether FFP was a direct attempt to create a protected environment, as some would argue," says Pearce, "or whether the protectionism was an accidental outcome of regulatory measures brought in to make football more financially sustainable, and you can debate that until the cows come home, the effect was a barrier to entry. Barriers were being put up, by design or accidentally, and the only way we could get through those barriers was a blitzkrieg of investment. That's exactly what it was."

It is not a coincidence that Manchester City's financial nadir was reached in the final year before the commencement of the initial two-year monitoring period for FFP in 2011-12 and 2012-13, with both public and private signals out of the European regulator at the time indicating that it was likely to be more lenient on clubs that were at least trending in the right direction.

"We're at the end of that period," said Cook privately in 2010. "The investment in the playing squad will slow down on the basis that we now feel we have a team that can compete with the best in the Premier League, and if you can compete with the best in the Premier League, the automatic outcome of that is competing in the Champions League. We will now adjust rather than rebuild our football team."

Rival clubs might question whether signings such as Edin Džeko [2011], Samir Nasri [2011] and Sergio Agüero [2011] represented mere adjustments, but there was no repeat of the broad summer spending sprees of 2009 and 2010. In the 2011 summer transfer window for example, Manchester City signed six players, sold six players, and put another 16 out on loan. The Club's net transfer spend in 2011-12 came in under £70 million, after topping £120 million in each of the previous three seasons, as the perennial price takers began to focus more intently on plans to expand the Club's ability to produce more world-class players of its own.

"The priority was to get the first team right," said Marwood privately in May 2011, "and I think that's where the majority of the focus and the resources have been positioned. We're now getting into a place where we can start to look at underpinning that with a successful youth development plan."

At the time, the twin pillars of that effort were the Club's plans to develop a new training campus in the vicinity of the City of Manchester Stadium [now Etihad

Stadium], and the adoption of a new Academy Development Plan that would reform the Club's approach to youth development.

These weren't entirely new initiatives. In December 2008, only three months after ADUG's acquisition of Manchester City, at the owner's directive the newly constituted board commissioned a mysterious initiative dubbed the 'World Leading Project [WLP].' This was the seed that would grow into what is now known as the City Football Academy [CFA].

"The World Leading Project was a conscious effort to step outside of the day-to-day running of the organisation, and to try to understand what great looked like in terms of the physical infrastructure needed to support a world-leading football organisation," explains Jon Stemp, who led the secretive project while overseeing a range of improvements to the Club's existing infrastructure. "We were improving and refurbishing almost every part of the Club, but that exercise had a short-term functional outcome. We felt we also needed to decouple ourselves from the day-to-day, to really think about a more transformative step change that the organisation would need to become world leading."

The first part of the exercise was an extensive research project to identify the key characteristics of a world-leading facility for the training and development of young footballers. In 2009, the Club conducted a vast fact-finding mission that involved studying the training facilities of 14 European football clubs and at least nine non-football entities to identify key learnings and best practices.

"The research activity for the World Leading Project was fundamentally about three things," says Stemp. "It was about looking at organisations, looking at their facilities, but also looking at their key people, and understanding how their knowledge and insights have shaped these environments. It was trying to understand whether there were common ingredients in each of these three parts of our research work."

More than anything, Stemp says the research highlighted the important relationship that exists between the philosophies and values of successful organisations and their physical infrastructure.

"Every successful sporting organisation we went to was different," he says. "They were all unique, and there was something about their organisation that made them who they were. When we came back, we looked at this ingredient time and time again, and whether it was Barcelona or Real Madrid, or the [Miami] Dolphins or

Manchester City break the British transfer record on deadline day, September 1st 2008, with the signing of Robinho for £32.5m

The front page of The Sun newspaper on September 3rd 2008

Manchester City's Academy at Platt Lane, 7 miles from the first team training complex at Carrington, October 2008

Before: Manchester City's Carrington Training Complex before its
rapid transformation in October 2008

After: Manchester City's Carrington Training Complex
after the upgrade in October 2008

Outgoing Chairman Thaksin Shinawatra raises Khaldoon Al Mubarak's
hand aloft at the City of Manchester Stadium, September 21st 2008

Premier League

More	Position	Club	Played	Won	Drawn	Lost	GF	GA	GD	Points	Form
∨	1	Liverpool	18	11	6	1	27	12	15	39	D D W D D
∨	2	Chelsea	18	11	5	2	36	7	29	38	D L W D D
∨	3	Aston Villa	18	10	4	4	30	20	10	34	D D W W W
∨	4	Manchester United	16	9	5	2	27	10	17	32	W D W W D
∨	5	Arsenal	18	9	4	5	30	21	9	31	L W W D D
∨	6	Hull City	18	7	6	5	27	31	-4	27	D D W D L
∨	7	Everton	18	7	5	6	23	25	-2	26	L W L W D
∨	8	Fulham	17	6	6	5	16	12	4	24	D D D D W
∨	9	Bolton Wanderers	18	7	2	9	22	24	-2	23	W W L L W
∨	10	Portsmouth	18	6	5	7	20	28	-8	23	D W D L L
∨	11	Wigan Athletic	17	6	4	7	21	20	1	22	D W W L W
∨	12	Newcastle United	18	5	7	6	24	25	-1	22	D D D W W
∨	13	Sunderland	18	6	3	9	21	26	-5	21	L L L W W
∨	14	Middlesbrough	18	5	5	8	17	27	-10	20	L D L D L
∨	15	Stoke City	18	5	5	8	17	30	-13	20	W D D D L
∨	16	Tottenham Hotspur	18	5	4	9	20	23	-3	19	W L W D L
∨	17	West Ham United	18	5	4	9	18	26	-8	19	W D L D L
∨	18	Manchester City	18	5	3	10	31	27	4	18	W L D L L
∨	19	Blackburn Rovers	18	4	4	10	20	34	-14	16	L L L L W
∨	20	West Bromwich Albion	18	4	3	11	14	33	-19	15	L L D L W

Manchester City sit in 18th place in the
table in December 2008

Brian Marwood, England capped, former Arsenal, Hull and Sheffield Wednesday winger, now City Football Group's Managing Director of Global Football

Gareth Barry chooses Manchester City over a number of interested clubs in June 2009, becoming the first major signing of the summer transfer window

Carlos Tevez crosses the city to sign for Manchester City in June 2009

Joleon Lescott joins Manchester City in August 2009
after protracted transfer negotiations with Everton

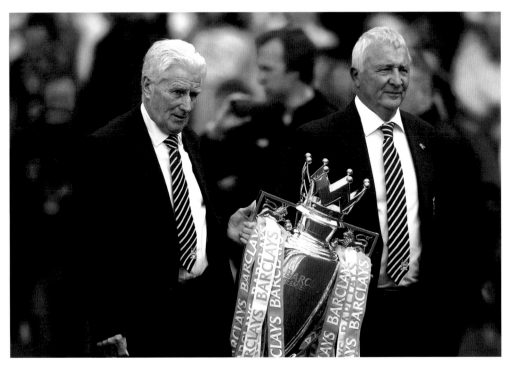

Mike Summerbee as Club Ambassador
with Tony Book in 2012

Mike Summerbee in action for
Manchester City in 1968

Roberto Mancini is unveiled as Manager of
Manchester City in December 2009

Mark Hughes coaches his final game as Manchester
City Manager in December 2009

Chief Communications Officer Vicky Kloss with Manager Roberto
Mancini, wearing the scarf she gave him before his first match

Patrick Vieira, who would be part of the City family for 8 years as a player, executive
and coach, joins Manchester City from Inter Milan in January 2010

David Silva, a player central to Manchester City's evolution over the last eight years, joins the Club from Valencia in June 2010

Yaya Touré with then CEO Garry Cook and Chief Football Administration Officer Brian Marwood following his signing in July 2010

His Highness Sheikh Mansour bin Zayed Al Nahyan watches Manchester City beat Liverpool at home in August 2010, pictured with Chairman Khaldoon Al Mubarak and then CEO Garry Cook

Yaya Touré scores the match-winner in the FA Cup semi-final at Wembley in April 2011, to take Manchester City to their first major cup final in three decades

Chairman Khaldoon Al Mubarak and Roberto Mancini
at Wembley in May 2011

Manchester City beat Stoke City in the FA Cup final in May 2011,
bringing the Club its first major piece of silverware in 35 years

Sergio Agüero, who would go on to become the highest goal scorer in Manchester City's history, joins the Club from Atlético Madrid in July 2011

Board Director John MacBeath becomes interim CEO of Manchester City in September 2011

Carlos Tevez on the bench in Munich on the night of his infamous
falling out with Manager Roberto Mancini in September 2011

Mario Balotelli at Old Trafford in October 2011 after scoring the first of his two
goals in the derby match Manchester City would go on to win 6-1

Vincent Kompany celebrates after scoring the match-winning goal against Manchester United in the crucial penultimate home game of the 2011-12 Premier League season

Roberto Mancini and Mark Hughes pitted against each other on the final day of the 2011-12 season, where Manchester City had to beat QPR to be crowned Premier League champions

Edin Džeko scores the pivotal equaliser in added time
against QPR on the final day of the 2011-12 season

Sergio Agüero scores in the 94th minute against QPR to clinch Manchester
City's first top flight league title in 44 years in May 2012

Joe Hart celebrates Manchester City's historic
Premier League triumph, May 2012

Manchester City Captain Vincent Kompany lifts the Premier
League trophy at the Etihad Stadium, May 2012

whoever it was, they all had a really strong philosophy that was out front and said, 'This is who we are.' It reaffirmed to us that successful organisations hold on to their values and their core identity, and those principles drive who they are and the way they behave, and it struck us that actually City already had its own philosophy and core values. It was about community. It was about being a club of the people. It was about acting in a really cohesive way to bring people together, and using the power of football for social good."

At the same time, ADUG and Manchester City commenced the process of quietly accumulating around 80 hectares of land in East Manchester. That land would one day make up the lion's share of what is now known as the Etihad Campus, under a ten-year, £400m partnership agreement signed between the Club and Etihad Airways in July 2011, which encompassed a range of commercial properties, including front-of-shirt sponsorship and naming rights to the Stadium and Campus [which houses the CFA].

"It was clear we needed to buy a lot of land around the Stadium to make sure we could do things that we didn't know we wanted to do yet," says Manchester City board member Marty Edelman, who commenced the land acquisition process on behalf of ADUG within months of its investment in Manchester City. "We wanted to keep it fairly secret because we didn't want the prices to skyrocket, and if people knew we were going to spend all this money on a training facility, then prices would go up."

"It was a challenging site to gather because there were lots of different ownerships on the site," explains Pete Bradshaw, "but when we drew it out we all came to the conclusion that if you could build an academy on the site we are on now, and have a junior academy, senior academy, Elite Development Squad, first team and stadium, all in line with each other, with some community facilities at one end, then you would create this street-to-stadium vision. It had to work practically as well, and there was just this incredible buzz about trying to achieve that."

ADUG found a powerful ally for the project in Manchester City Council [owner of the City of Manchester Stadium and therefore Manchester City's landlord], and in particular, its then Chief Executive, Sir Howard Bernstein.

"I met Sir Howard and Sir Richard [Leese, Leader of Manchester City Council], who are very human and very direct and incredibly smart and very open," recalls

Edelman, "and rather than walking into an environment which was hostile or neutral, it was an environment that said, 'We don't know a lot about you, but we want to like you, so help us,' and it was great. The first time I came to Manchester, we had dinner with them and started talking right away about the kinds of things we have ended up doing."

"I didn't have any grand design on that first day that we should develop a Man Life [Manchester Life] proposition, that we should look at the health and performance issue [Manchester Institute of Health & Performance], that we should have the CFA," says Bernstein, who was knighted for his services to Manchester in 2003, "but what we wanted was a partner, because the football club was always going to be an essential platform, an essential ingredient, of that wider regeneration story."

At that time, East Manchester could use all the help that it could get.

"If we go back to the 1970's and maybe the very beginning of the 1980's, this was still a very active industrial part of the city," says Bradshaw. "That wasn't that long ago really, but by the middle of the 1980's it had all gone. The coal mine had closed down in the 70's. The power station closed down for demolition. Factories had all disappeared. The jobs went. The neighbourhood had deteriorated. There were no schools in the area. The population disappeared, and those that were left found it difficult to find work. That stayed the same for several decades. The Commonwealth Games [in 2002] clearly was a catalyst, but actually more important than that was the legacy that came out of it, and one of the greatest achievements of that legacy is the CFA, because we transformed an area of the most dreadful dereliction and pollution."

Bernstein and the Council were quick to recognise that the arrival of ADUG represented a once-in-a-generation opportunity to revive their longstanding ambitions for the East Manchester area.

"We always had an idea of a campus," says Bernstein. "We called it SportCity [built for the Commonwealth Games]. The proposition was, how can sport became an engine of economic growth? How can sport became an engine of personal achievement? How can it drive different behaviours and priorities within the wider community? How can we use it to induce new investment and trading opportunities? We always had that vision, and I picked up that overall approach from the Barcelona Olympics in '92, and how sport became an engine of economic growth for Barcelona."

In 2009, Manchester City Council entered into an initial Memorandum of Understanding with Manchester City Football Club to explore opportunities for the two parties to work together on a range of new initiatives in East Manchester. In 2010, a fully-fledged Joint Development Board [involving Manchester City Football Club, Manchester City Council, and New East Manchester Ltd.] was established to facilitate collaboration on the commercial development of their respective landholdings and on the economic regeneration of the area. At that time, the three entities owned a combined total of 200 acres of land in the vicinity of the City of Manchester Stadium, including land that had been acquired by ADUG and Manchester City since the takeover.

In December 2011, Manchester City received unanimous planning approval from Manchester City Council to proceed with the development of the CFA, with the Club donating 5.5 acres of land for the development of a range of community facilities, including a new leisure centre and sixth form college.

"There was real vision from Sir Howard and Sir Richard Leese," says Stemp. "I think the Council knew that the football club had new ownership and that new ownership had significant resources, and the City Council was smart enough to say, 'We should think about working with these guys beyond the football club.'"

For its part, ADUG chose to align its own plans with the Council's existing vision for the area.

"When I brought in [Uruguayan architect] Rafael Viñoly to start helping us think about master planning, we immediately linked ourselves to the East Manchester Strategic Regeneration Framework, so that we weren't an island," recalls Edelman. "That was very important to Sheikh Mansour and Khaldoon's view of what we should be."

Although he had spent his entire career at the Council, famously washing cups on his first day before rising to Chief Executive 27 years later in 1998, Sir Howard Bernstein wasn't the classic government bureaucrat that ADUG officials had expected.

"I've not met too many government officials that are as entrepreneurial as he is," says Al Mubarak. "I deal with officials all over the world, and most of the time it's about them winning and the other side losing. It's about being rigid and structured in a way that makes things difficult to get done. Sir Howard's the opposite. He always looks for these win-win scenarios. What's best for Manchester, and for investors like ADUG or Manchester City, what can be done that's win-win?"

As ADUG and Manchester City continued collecting land for the proposed new training campus, in 2011, the board also approved a new Academy Development Plan. Based on an analysis of 12 football entities [including a mix of clubs and national bodies] and four non-football entities, the 91-page document made 38 detailed recommendations to transform the Club's approach to the selection, training and development of young footballers.

In 2011-12, the Club recruited 20 new players from more than seven countries into its youth development system. In July 2012, the Manchester City Academy was granted Category One status under the Premier League's new Elite Player Performance Plan [EPPP] which, among other things, would enable it to cast a wider net when scouting and recruiting promising young players from within the UK.

After three years of aggressive spending in the transfer market, the Club and its ownership could now see much greater long-term value in the investments being made in its training facilities and youth development capabilities. Manager Roberto Mancini had also shown a willingness to tap into the Club's youth development pipeline, giving 14 Academy players first team debuts in the 2010-11 and 2011-12 seasons [on top of the four Academy players he gave debuts to in his first four-and-a-half months in charge in 2009-10].

"The question is, and we've talked about it," said Cook privately in 2010, "'If I gave you £150 million tomorrow, would you go out and buy five players?' The answer is, 'No. I'd build the new training centre for youth development.' Now, it's about building infrastructure. We're on track. We're doing what we always said we were going to do. Nobody ever believed us."

CHAPTER 8:

SEEING RED

The first Manchester derby took place in 1881 when St Mark's [West Gorton], which would eventually become Manchester City in 1894, played Newton Heath LYR, which would later become Manchester United in 1902. The two sides officially faced off for the first time as Manchester City and Manchester United on Christmas Day, 1902. Over the next century, the competition between these two local clubs would grow into one of the world's greatest sporting rivalries.

"The Manchester derby's always been important," says football historian Gary James, "but what happened during the late 80's and the 90's and early 2000's is that Manchester United played it down, particularly Alex Ferguson [appointed Manager of Manchester United in 1986], because his focus was on matching Liverpool's achievements, or eclipsing them."

Manchester City didn't have any bigger fish to fry.

"From the Manchester City point of view, nothing changed in terms of the derby," says James. "It still mattered as it always mattered. The derby didn't happen every season [with Manchester City relegated from the Premier League in 1996 and 2001], and the Liverpool-United rivalry got more intense, but the Manchester derby was still the same. It just wasn't getting national or international attention. By the time of the takeover, City had constantly seen United as its big rival, and in many ways there was nothing else to play for each season other than beating them."

James isn't exaggerating.

"The day I joined the Club, I went to the retail store and asked them what the best-selling item was," says former CEO, Garry Cook, "and they said, 'The DVD from 2007-08 when we beat United at home and away, which is all that really matters!'"

The outcome of the derby had never stopped counting on the streets of Manchester.

"When I was a kid, Manchester City were Mike Summerbee, Colin Bell, Francis Lee," recalls Sir Howard Bernstein. "They were at the top of their game. Champions in '68. In the 70's we enjoyed a continued renaissance. The 80's and 90's were pretty awful, and that coincides of course with United winning championships almost on an annual basis, so the dynamics within the city were very clear and divisive actually. United were top dogs. City had two games a season really. Our redemption was just about beating United twice a year."

"It's like two gladiators getting into a ring and somebody wins," says Manchester City legend and Club Ambassador, Mike Summerbee. "I played here years ago when Bobby Charlton and Denis Law played [for Manchester United], and to play in a derby game is everything. It means so much. It's about the 22 players on the field, the 11 players for City and the 11 players for United, doing what they can to make sure that the people who support them can go to work on a Monday morning with a smile on their face. Even now, if we get beaten in a derby, at the end of the day I am depressed, and I don't even play anymore."

"When you are a local boy you know what it means," says assistant coach, Brian Kidd, who grew up in Collyhurst in the inner-city of Manchester and has played and coached at both Manchester United and Manchester City at various points in a unique career. "The derby game is very special. It's about bragging rights, is it not?"

That's why many local observers saw the ADUG takeover of Manchester City, and its transformational impact on the Club's spending power, almost entirely through the lens of the City-United rivalry. However, Manchester City and ADUG officials generally downplay the extent to which Manchester United served as a singular benchmark for the Club during this period.

"Actually, I hadn't even been to [Manchester United's home ground] Old Trafford," says Marty Edelman, who oversaw large parts of the Club's land acquisition and infrastructure strategies at board level. "We didn't want to be confined by others' experiences. We were motivated by doing something new and different, and that's really what we were focused on."

"We're too big as a club to worry about what Manchester United or anybody else is doing," said Summerbee privately in May 2011. "We're going one way, and that's up, and we're doing it in a gentlemanly way and we're doing it in a friendly way."

For the record, Summerbee then proceeded to disparage Manchester United in a friendly way for the next two to three minutes.

Board member John MacBeath says Manchester United served a limited purpose as a competitive benchmark at the time.

"I can honestly tell you I've never woken up in the morning and worried about what Manchester United were doing," he says, "but what I have done is woken up in the morning and thought, what are we going to do with Manchester City and how do we take this forward? And football's like any other business. Benchmarking is tremendously important. You have to know who your competitors are. You have to know what your competitors' strengths are. You have to try and replicate those strengths, but differentiate yourself from them sufficiently, to enable yourself to deliver a better result. I mean, that's just ABC of business. I think the fact that we share the city with them, and that they were so predominant in the early days, was a useful wake up call, but they were never going to help us. We had to do our own thing."

However, one former footballer in Manchester City's ranks took a different view to some of his colleagues.

"I would purposely drive past Old Trafford every day," says Brian Marwood. "People would say 'What are you doing that for?', and I'd say, 'That reminds me of what good looks like. That building is a monument to success. We have to create that, and I want something to remind me of that every day.'"

In hindsight, there was something prophetic about the habit. As fate would have it, the route to each major milestone for the newly-resurgent Manchester City – branded the "noisy neighbours" by Sir Alex Ferguson within a year of the ADUG takeover – would require them to get past Manchester United.

The first real opportunity for Manchester City to win a trophy in the ADUG era came in the 2009-10 League Cup, but the Club had to beat Manchester United over two legs in order to make the final. On 19 January 2010, Manchester City won the first leg at home in a heated exchange dominated by ex-United player, Carlos Tevez, who scored two goals and taunted his former club from the pitch.

In his 2012 book, 'My Decade In The Premier League,' Manchester United striker Wayne Rooney described his side's mindset in the lead-up to the second game.

"By the time the second leg comes around we're really up for it," he wrote. "City are talking a lot before the game about their plans and ambitions. They're looking to qualify for the Champions League, especially after spending a lot of money in the summer. We know we have to put them in their place. We know we have to win."[9]

Manchester United bounced back, winning the tie 4-3 on aggregate courtesy of a Rooney goal in the 93rd minute of the second game [which ended 3-1], handing Roberto Mancini his first big loss at Manchester City, and halting the Club's growing momentum. Adding insult to injury, Manchester City would fail to qualify for the UEFA Champions League at the end of the season.

"The League Cup semi-final against United in 2010 was crucial," says James, "because it was our first semi-final since 1981, and it was against United. The first leg was fantastic and we thought we'd won it, and in the second leg we got knocked out and we lost it. All such things happened at Old Trafford. It was a bad day and it was very much a case of United putting City back into the box. That's it. You're never going to overcome United."

Rooney would be there to twist the knife yet again in February 2011, settling a tense Premier League derby 2-1 with an acrobatic goal in the 78th minute. Sir Alex Ferguson would later describe it as the best goal scored during his 26 years as Manchester United Manager. Rooney would declare it to be the best of his career. Manchester United had now won five of the six Premier League games played between the two sides since the ADUG takeover in 2008. The sixth had been a draw.

"That was a special game," recalls Vincent Kompany, "because we were actually really good in that game, and Wayne didn't have his best of games. He's played some good games, especially in the derbies, and this wasn't his best, but because he's a top player, out of nothing he pulls a bicycle kick, they win 2-1, and we're sent packing and they've got the three points. But, you know, you go to these places, they've got great players, and it can happen."

The stunning match winner was a humbling blow, but Yaya Touré says the reaction of Rooney and his team mates was revealing.

"When Rooney scored that goal, and he ran to the corner, and all his team mates went with him, and they celebrated like they were playing against Barcelona, at that time I felt like United had started to fear City," he says.

He likens the situation to a sibling rivalry.

"It's like me and my brother," explains Touré. "If I always beat him, day after day, after that you don't have a feeling, you don't have a happiness, because you know you're going to beat him. You don't have to be so happy or proud of yourself, and when Rooney scored the goal, all his team mates they were celebrating like crazy. It was a beautiful goal, but the feeling I had was, we're going to go on top of them, because they take us very seriously now, and they could see City was coming."

Manchester City would get another shot two months later, this time in the semi-final of the 2010-11 FA Cup at Wembley Stadium on 16 April 2011, where once again they would have to beat Manchester United for the right to even play for a trophy.

Before kick-off that day, midfielder Patrick Vieira, already the winner of three FA Cups, asked Manager Roberto Mancini to leave the dressing room so that he could address his team mates directly.

"I think that was a massive part of the game," says Gareth Barry, "because we were playing United. The power that they've had in the city after what they'd done in the previous decade was pretty daunting, and in what they'd achieved in terms of what [Manchester] City had. He just made a big point of, 'Just think of the players we've got in the dressing room and who they've got in theirs. There's nothing in it. On our day we can beat them. We've got as much talent. Forget the past because it's on the day,' sort of thing. He made a great speech that still sticks in my memory and turned maybe the thinking and mentality of the players going out there before the game."

"I don't remember what he said but I just remember staring at him like he was God," says an honest Joleon Lescott, recalling the dramatic scene before the game. "It was like... 'Wow.' He must have agreed it with Mancini, because Pat's not disrespectful, but it was needed."

It isn't the moment that stands out for everybody.

"I can't remember that," says Kompany, "but I remember that we had a big argument at halftime. We had a team with big characters. I think the big difference between the team of today [2018] and the team of then is, I think today we've become this kind of swarm where everybody shares responsibilities, shares effort, and everything that goes with it. But, a lot of the success we had in the early days was based on big characters in big moments making the difference. So, I had a pretty hefty argument with Yaya at halftime. We don't argue a lot, but it was all because [Manchester United midfielder] Paul Scholes was running the game."

Little did Scholes know but he was also dominating discussion in the Manchester City dressing room.

"We couldn't get close to him," recalls Kompany, "and I kind of pointed that out to Yaya in my own terms, that we needed to close in there. Yaya replied that it was something else that was going wrong, and then it was going back and forth. And I do think that these were the things that got us going back in those days. We needed something to spark. Like a fight in a training session, or an argument, and big personalities always rose to the challenge. It wasn't the things you maybe write about what perfection is, but it was big characters standing up to achieve a goal, and that happened in the United game."

Two of the biggest characters to stand up that day were goalkeeper Joe Hart, who made a number of crucial saves, and Yaya Touré, who scored the game's only goal in the 52nd minute. Although he may not have known it, Hart played a small role in the match winning goal too.

"In the past," recalls Touré, "when I was trying to shoot, Joe Hart had told me, 'When the keeper is coming, he always makes himself bigger, to close the goal, and what you have to do, you have to put it between his two legs or between his hand and his shoulder.' And when [Edwin] van der Sar was coming, I was thinking in my head, 'I will put it between his legs.'"

Replays show Touré deftly slotting the ball between the advancing keeper's legs on its way into the back of the net. Manchester City held on to win the game 1-0 and book its place in the FA Cup final.

"I think that day changed everything," says James. "If City had been beaten, no matter how it had been beaten, even if it had been a fantastic United performance or an awful City performance, it would have killed us. It would have done, but because City won and Yaya Touré scored that goal, that was the point when things were different. That was the point when we knew, City still might not win a trophy, but there wasn't something to stop us. It was up to us."

"You never want to lose to United because there is that City pride," says Marwood. "They had been so successful and we were just beginning to emerge, so that was a huge day for us and one that I'll remember for a lot of years. I always felt there have been moments in time here where the Club has gone to another level. I think that was a moment in time. It was a big occasion, and that could have got to a number of players, but it didn't."

Manchester City would subsequently go on to beat Stoke City in the 130th FA Cup final at Wembley Stadium on 14 May 2011.

Just as he had done in the semi-final, Yaya Touré scored the game's only goal [in the 74th minute].

"It was not the best goal in the world, but it was going to make the Club go forward," he says of the powerful left-footed strike that secured Manchester City its first major piece of silverware in 35 years.

Watching on from the stands that day were members of the Club's last FA Cup-winning side from 1969, including Francis Lee, Mike Summerbee and Colin Bell. 24 minutes into the game, the Manchester City fans at Wembley turned their backs on the action and did 'the Poznan' in tribute to the late Neil Young's match-winning goal in the 1969 final.

"Not many players have played in FA Cup finals," says Summerbee, who sent in the cross that led to Young's goal in 1969. "Some players have never played in a cup final. That's how special it is to play in it and win it. I played in one when we beat Leicester 1-0, and to be sat in the stands with some of the players that played at that particular time, watching the new Manchester City, Sheikh Mansour's team, taking over and winning the first trophy, was something. It was very emotional."

"It was almost like we could not believe it," says Cook. "There was no reason for us not to believe it, because it was inevitable that it was going to happen, but then you come out of the Stadium and grown men are crying, old people are coming up to you, shaking your hand and saying, 'Thank you very much. I never thought I would see this day. I never thought my kids were going to see it.' Brian Kidd said to me after the game, 'After you have won the first one, you win loads, but it is winning that first one, you have got to win the first one.'"

Looking back on that successful FA Cup campaign today, most Manchester City players and officials still point to the semi-final win over Manchester United as the most important game of all, even though it wasn't the one that ended with a trophy presentation.

"From the moment we beat United, we knew," says Kompany. "We celebrated almost just as much when we beat United in the semi-final as when we beat Stoke in the final. And as soon as that happened, the final for us was never going to be a loss. And Yaya did his thing at the right time again, but I never doubted this."

"I don't remember too much about the final," admits Marwood, who had signed most of the players wearing blue that day, "but we won it. We got the job done. And to beat United, then to beat Stoke, and for it to be the first trophy for 35 years, it was like this belief was beginning to grow. All of the things that had gone on for the previous two-and-a-half years had been about growing and developing and creating something, but in the end you have to win a trophy. You have to show people that you can win."

Later that night, Manchester City officials celebrated on the ground floor of the Mandarin Oriental Hotel in London, where CEO Garry Cook presented the Chairman with an engraved, full-sized replica of the FA Cup to take back to Sheikh Mansour in Abu Dhabi. Cook joked that he had no idea how he would have disposed of the item if the team had failed to win. The arrival of cup-winning Manager, Roberto Mancini, was marked with an impromptu rendition of 'Mancini, oh, oh, oh.'

Speaking with Chris Bailey for CityTV the following morning [just days after Manchester City had also secured a top four finish in the 2010-11 Premier League], the Chairman, Khaldoon Al Mubarak, made clear that the Club and its owner had their sights set on much bigger things in 2011-12.

"This week marks an important step forward," said Al Mubarak, "but it's only a step forward. Our ambitions are obviously much bigger than that. Now, we are in the Champions League, but we need to perform. That's a big challenge. We've won the FA Cup. That's great, but I believe there are more cups to win. And being fourth in the Premier League is a good accomplishment, but we want to win the League."

Manchester City entered the 2011-12 season with high hopes and a decent chance of doing just that.

CHAPTER 9:

THE
TURBULENCE

Manchester City got off to a flying start in the 2011-12 season with three wins from three matches in the opening rounds of the Premier League. The Club was also gearing up for its long-awaited debut in the UEFA Champions League. It was away from the pitch where Manchester City's most promising season in decades would first begin to unravel, with the Club losing its CEO before it lost a single game.

A story that first appeared in The Sun on 5 September 2011 alleged that months earlier, Manchester City CEO Garry Cook had accidentally sent an offensive email to the now late Dr Anthonia Onuoha, the mother and agent of defender Nedum Onuoha, which made reference to her battle with cancer.

An investigation by the Club concluded there was foundation to the allegations and Cook resigned on 9 September 2011.

"Garry's departure from Manchester City was an incredibly sad moment," says Simon Pearce, the board director that had worked most closely with Cook over the preceding three years. "He gave everything he had to the transformation of City during his tenure. This was a man who could have walked away with the entire value of his contract when we took over the Club, and he chose to stay because the opportunity was what he had signed up for. City meant that much to him.

Garry's contributions were essential to creating the foundations on which we have continued to build ever since."

Following Cook's departure, Manchester City director John MacBeath, a former senior executive at BAE Systems, was asked to step in as interim CEO. What was originally pitched to him as a four-to-six-week gig would end up lasting for over a year.

"I took over an organisation that was highly functional," says MacBeath, looking back on the appointment, "and an organisation that had a lot of good people in it. So, whilst I won't pretend that I wouldn't have done things differently, had I known I was coming in for a full year, there wasn't a whole lot that you needed to really get after. We were executing against a long-term plan. We got the Club's losses reduced to just under the hundred million mark [£97.9] in 2011-12, so there was a cost control element that had to be enforced. And of course, I had to make sure that regardless of what had happened, the show would go on."

Relatively reserved by nature, the interim boss planned to conduct that show largely from backstage. However, it wasn't to be. Two weeks later, Carlos Tevez and Roberto Mancini would have a bitter, pitch side falling out in Munich [the Manager accusing the player of refusing to go on as a substitute in a UEFA Champions League game, the player later accusing the Manager of treating him "like a dog"], and just like that, the tensions that had been quietly simmering away within the Manchester City squad for months dramatically boiled over on one of football's biggest stages.

"I was on the pitch at the time so I had no idea what was happening on the bench in that part of the field," said Sergio Agüero in his 2014 book, 'Born to Rise.' "It was obviously very heated in the dressing room after the game and Mancini was going mad at Tevez telling him to go back to Argentina and then he told some other players to go back to their countries."[10]

The travelling Manchester City delegation, seated on the same side of the ground as the players' dugout, hadn't seen the embarrassing incident playing out beneath them as it happened.

"I was in Munich that night," recalls MacBeath, "and I remember it, because I came out of the seating area where we'd watched the game from, and Brian Marwood was beside me. Brian took his phone out of his pocket and he said, 'John, I think something's happened.' He had dozens of messages. And it then transpired that, I think a row that had been brewing for a few days between Carlos and Roberto had blown up when Roberto claimed he'd refused to play that night."

"I believe there had been a number of fall-outs between Carlitos and Mancini in the past so this was the straw that broke the camel's back," said Agüero in his 2014 book. "Tevez can have a short fuse at times, just as Mancini did, so it was perhaps inevitable that it would explode at some point."[11]

"By the time we get off a plane back from Germany," recalls Marwood, "I think we landed at one or two in the morning, we walked through the arrivals hall and there was press everywhere. It was a media frenzy."

"You kind of deal with that," says MacBeath. "Then you think, 'Okay, let's find out what really happened.' So, I got Simon Cliff, the lawyer, and Gilly King, our then head of HR, with a firm of lawyers here in Manchester, to carry out a Board of Inquiry effectively, because until we could find out exactly what had happened, you couldn't really work out what the appropriate course of action was."

"We put a very formalised process in place to investigate it," says Simon Cliff, now CFG's General Counsel, who had come a long way from dealing with mergers and acquisitions in the City of London just three years earlier. "It was quite legally-led, and it escalated quite quickly into this public dispute of briefings and counter briefings, but then also an escalating legal dispute of letters going backwards and forwards between his lawyers and us, and some external lawyers we brought in to advise us. I remember going around to his house in Alderley Edge to interview him as part of the investigation and there were cameras outside the gate."

"And the problem was that we had the whole world acting as judge and jury on the basis of television footage that was taken from the other side of the stadium," says MacBeath. "So, first of all, we had to find out what had gone on, and what went on that night was just the manifestation of the breakdown of a relationship between the Manager and a player."

Tevez was suspended for two weeks as the matter was investigated. Following a disciplinary hearing, he was then fined four weeks' wages for his role in the incident [with the fine halved following the intervention of the Professional Footballers Association]. The investigation was unable to substantiate the specific allegation that Tevez had actually refused to play that night, but did find him in breach of his contract in other ways. The distinction meant little to Mancini, who was not yet prepared to welcome Tevez back, and instructed the player to train on his own or with members of the Club's Elite Development Squad.

"It was still festering," says MacBeath. "There was still a bit of point scoring going on."

Tevez would soon make matters worse, allegedly travelling to Argentina without permission during the international break in November 2011, and setting off another protracted disciplinary issue for the Club – including its football, HR, communications and legal departments – to deal with in the middle of the season.

"We were caught in a situation where we could have spent all day, and every day, agonising over Carlos Tevez," explains MacBeath. "And this organisation is too big, and the job in front of us was too important, for us to allow that to happen. So, at Simon Pearce's suggestion, he said 'Look, let's cut to the chase here. Let's do a call every morning, where everybody can dial in and participate, and then we'll go away and deal with any actions that come out of that, and we'll get on with the rest of our day jobs as well.' And I think that was a great example of just trying to understand and contain a problem, rather than letting the problem take over everything."

While many in the pundit class thought Tevez deserved to be jettisoned around this time, MacBeath says that would have been akin to the Club cutting off its nose to spite its face.

"We had a very expensive footballer, carrying very significant value on the balance sheet, and nobody was going to win if his career had come to an end at that point," says MacBeath. "Certainly not us, because we were faced with a massive financial write off, and actually, we would have been seen to have failed as an organisation, because we wouldn't have been able to recover a situation that had developed."

The prospect of a move to AC Milan in the final week of the transfer window in January 2012 was effectively quashed when the Manchester City Chairman, Khaldoon Al Mubarak, bluntly told UAE-based newspaper, The National, that the Club had no intention of letting the player go cheaply in order to put an end to the affair.

"As things stand AC Milan isn't an option for Carlos Tevez," Al Mubarak told The National's Kevin Affleck. "Carlos remains a player with contractual obligations to

Manchester City for the next two and a half seasons. Unless we receive an offer that we deem appropriate, the terms of his contract will be enforced."[12]

It was an uncharacteristically public intervention from the understated Chairman that underscored the growing resolve of Manchester City and ADUG that they would not be railroaded or taken for fools by others in the game.

Left unsold in the January transfer window, Tevez returned to Manchester in February 2012. It was estimated at the time that the player had already cost himself more than £9m during his relatively brief tenure at Manchester City.

However, even in the absence of Tevez, Manchester City had continued to rack up wins in the Premier League, with none more memorable than a 6-1 thrashing of Manchester United at Old Trafford on 23 October 2011.

At the game that day, Vicky Kloss left her seat in the stands with the score at 3-1 to prepare for the team's post-match media commitments. As a lifelong Manchester City fan, conditioned to anticipate the worst, she says she still feared what might come next. However, by the time Kloss had got downstairs, Manchester City had scored again [via Edin Džeko in the 89th minute], making it 4-1 against a 10-man United.

They weren't done yet.

"I got to the mouth of the tunnel just in time to see a fifth goal scored," recalls Kloss, "but I am surrounded by United staff, so of course you have got to be really dignified about it, and then we scored a sixth and I am like, 'I am in dream world, this is insane,' and I want to scream with joy but I can't, because to celebrate wildly right there, right then, would be highly inappropriate!"

The Manchester City fans in the stands that day, and a large swathe of neutrals watching all over England, felt no such compunction.

"It was just euphoria," says Kloss. "No one could believe it. Roberto was as cool as you like. He was fantastic. Later that day I got a message from my husband [a Manchester United supporter]. We were supposed to be going together after the game to take our kids to Wales to have a few days together, and he texted me and just said, 'We will go in two separate cars.'

He wasn't kidding.

"That is exactly what happened," says a laughing Kloss, "and I did not mind at all because I spent my entire journey on the way to Wales phoning City fans, and my brother, and my Dad, going 'Oh my God.' So yes, Old Trafford was pretty stunned into silence."

Mancini's side would remain undefeated in the Premier League until losing 2-1 to Chelsea at Stamford Bridge on 12 December 2011. That loss came five days after the Club was knocked out in the Group Stage of the UEFA Champions League, despite winning half of its six games and accruing a points tally [10] that would have been enough to progress through almost any other group in the competition. However, the team rebounded strongly from these two setbacks, winning 10 of its next 14 Premier League games, including striking back against Chelsea [2-1] at home on 21 March 2012, in a match that featured the return of Carlos Tevez.

In fact, the wheels never completely came off at any stage during the 38-game Premier League season, but with back-to-back draws against Stoke City and Sunderland at the end of March 2012, the stalling Manchester City relinquished top spot in the table to the resilient Manchester United, who had brushed off their 6-1 humbling in October 2011 to remain squarely in the race for the title.

Despite leaving Manchester City in second place, Assistant Coach Brian Kidd says he always had a feeling that the draw against Sunderland [clawed back from a 3-1 deficit with five minutes remaining] on 31 March 2012 could turn out to be important.

"When we was 3-1 down against Sunderland, I had turned around and said, 'If we do not get a point out of this game, we are done for.' You must take something out of the games," says Kidd. "We pulled it back to 3-3, and then where I live I went in the local butchers, and they are big United fans, and they said to me 'Oh, 3-3,' and I turned around and said, and I genuinely meant it, 'That could turn out a great point come the end of the season.'"

According to Kidd, his butchers would later admit to him that after he had walked out of their shop that day, seemingly happy with a point against Sunderland, they had unanimously declared him to be both "daft" and "loony."

"That was the game I felt that if we had got beat we would not have won the League," says Kidd.

However, things would get even worse before they got better.

A week later, Manchester City lost 1-0 away to Arsenal on 8 April 2012, leaving itself eight points adrift of Manchester United with six rounds to play. Importantly, one of those games was a Manchester derby in the third-last game of the season on 30 April 2012, leaving three unanswered points up for grabs. Those points wouldn't be enough on their own, but they offered second-placed Manchester City a sliver of hope that the gap could still be closed.

In an interview with CityTV at the end of the season, Al Mubarak recalled visiting the away dressing room at Emirates Stadium immediately after the potentially devastating loss to Arsenal, and speaking with Manager, Roberto Mancini.

"We both looked at each other, and I think both of us had this moment," he said. "Let's take it one game at a time. We still can pull it off. But, let's take the pressure off everyone. Let's take the pressure off the team. Let's take the pressure off the players. That was a tough loss. It was a big let-down. But we have five more games to go, and if we win them all, with a bit of luck, we can still pull it off."

CHAPTER 10:

THE TRIUMPH

After going down to Arsenal, Manchester City surged out of North London with a vengeance, defeating West Bromwich Albion [4-0], Norwich City [6-1] and Wolverhampton Wanderers [2-0] in its next three games. Meanwhile, a Manchester United loss to Wigan [0-1] and dramatic late draw with Everton [4-4] meant that a City win in the Manchester derby on 30 April 2012 would bring the two sides level, with Manchester City ahead on goal difference. A loss would almost certainly put the title out of reach.

Speaking to the media two days before the match, Manager Roberto Mancini paid his respects to Manchester City's opponents while insisting the title was still Manchester United's to lose.

"I have a big respect for United because, for me, they are the best team here [in England], and maybe in Europe, with Barca and Real Madrid, but I think that Monday will be a different game, because it will be a derby," he said. "They have fantastic players. They have incredible spirit. I don't know what could happen [on] Monday."

He said he didn't anticipate negative tactics from Sir Alex Ferguson.

"For them, I think that a draw would be a good result," said Mancini, with Manchester United still three points ahead in the table, "but I don't feel that a team like them can play for a draw. I don't think that they have this mentality. Like us. We want to win, always, but I don't know if it's possible."

Ferguson would later provide an insight into his own thinking about the match in his autobiography.

"I knew the City game was bound to be tough and I thought they would play to kill the game, slow the pace down, give fouls away in our half and move the ball to Nasri and Silva to dribble with," he wrote. "By then, City were versed in such clever tactics."[13]

As it happened, the only goal of the night would come from the head of Manchester City captain Vincent Kompany, whose powerful celebration encapsulated the release of an array of feelings.

"I think that's the game with the most pressure on it that I've ever been in," says Kompany. "I'm good at dealing with pressure, so I was kind of comfortable still, but it was insane, because it was a midweek game, so everyone was watching it. It was United versus City. It was basically for the title. And with all the stories of City bottling it in the last minute or the last game, I think you can almost see it on my face after the goal, this..."

He searches for the words to describe it.

"...it's not anger, or frustration, but it's definitely pent up emotion that comes out, because you want to almost rebel against this image. You want to rebel against what everybody thinks this is going to turn out to be. That game was fantastic because obviously we scored the goal, which happened to be me, but we didn't concede one shot on target that game, against Manchester United, title contenders, and that to me was powerful in terms of how you react in big moments."

The 1-0 win drew Manchester City even with Manchester United on points, but with a virtually insurmountable lead on goal difference, largely thanks to that 6-1 drubbing in the October 2011 derby. All Manchester City had to do was win their last two games [against Newcastle away and QPR at home] in order to be crowned Premier League champions.

"And we still nearly threw it away," says a rueful Kompany.

After beating Newcastle 2-0 via a Yaya Touré brace at St James Park on 6 May 2012, soon the only thing that stood between Manchester City and the title was a struggling QPR, which would be fighting to avoid relegation on the final day of the season on 13 May 2012.

There were ghosts of seasons past all around the ground that day, from [former Manchester City Manager, now QPR Manager] Mark Hughes on the touchline, former Manchester City players [now QPR players] Joey Barton and Nedum

Onuoha on the pitch, and the decades of disappointment that had been burned into the calloused hearts of the Manchester City faithful in the stands.

"It's a huge game for Manchester City," said Hughes in his pre-match press conference, acutely aware that a tendency for failure in the most unlikely of circumstances ran deep in the history of his former club. "Make no bones about it. And if we can be in a situation where we're still very much in the game, and our future is still in our own hands, then maybe, just maybe, City might get a little bit nervous about the situation they find themselves in, and who knows? Stranger things have happened."

Stranger things did happen.

After leading 1-0 at the break courtesy of a Pablo Zabaleta goal in the 39th minute, Manchester City inexplicably let QPR back in the game, cheaply giving up an equaliser in the 48th minute. Then, after QPR midfielder Joey Barton was shown a red card for striking Carlos Tevez [before remarkably attacking Sergio Agüero on his way off the pitch], it was ten-man QPR that took an unlikely lead through a James Mackie header in the 66th minute, putting the visitors ahead 2-1. At that time, there were still 24 minutes on the clock, but despite its extra man, a stunned Manchester City seemed unable to strike back. It looked for all money like it wasn't going to happen.

"There was a numbness that I will never forget," says Manchester City Chairman, Khaldoon Al Mubarak, as he recalls watching the Club's title hopes slipping away before his eyes. "You know, the last ten minutes of that game, I was numb, because I was in two worlds. I was looking at this, and I couldn't believe that it was happening. And part of me was saying, 'We will win. We're going to find a way. It's impossible that we're not going to win the League today.' So, what was going through 60 per cent of my head was, 'Don't worry. It's going to work out.' And, don't forget, United were playing at the same time [against Sunderland], so in my head, I'm thinking 'Okay, let's tie the game, maybe they'll tie, and we'll win anyway.' Even when it got into the last minute, still in my heart, 60 per cent I would say, was saying, 'We'll tie. Maybe we still win the League that way.'"

And the other 40?

"40 per cent was saying, 'How am I going to deal with the aftermath of this?'" says Al Mubarak. "I was actually playing it out in my mind, 'Okay, what do I need to say?

What do I need to do once that referee blows that whistle, to get that team to win the League next year? Because this could go into meltdown.' So, my brain was kind of torn between these two spaces, between conviction, belief and hope, and measured thinking about what I would need to do, all in the span of those last ten minutes."

Captain Vincent Kompany agrees that a failure in those circumstances would have cast a long shadow.

"It makes me sick to even talk about it," he says, when asked to contemplate what would have happened if things had turned out differently, "but I think we would have gone into hiding for two months. It would have been a stain, really, because we did so many great things that season. You know, coming back at all was in itself a short miracle, because we were so far behind in terms of getting back to United's level. But then, winning against United the way we did it, beating Newcastle away, which was a top team at that time as well, and then throwing it away against a team that's fighting for relegation at home would have been a catastrophe. I can't even describe it. I don't know where the belief would have come from for anything else after that."

It was still 2-1 at the end of 90 minutes. At that hopeless moment, overcoming Manchester United still meant overcoming QPR, and overcoming QPR now meant scoring two goals in five minutes of added time, and doing that meant overcoming the palpable sense of disappointment and betrayal that had descended on the Etihad Stadium.

"I just remember seeing the clock go to 90 minutes," says Brian Marwood. "I was thinking, 'I just can't believe this. I can't believe this has happened. Why has this happened now?' There was so much that went into that year. The Carlos stuff. Roberto putting the team together. How hard we had worked behind the scenes because we could see that it was becoming a little bit divisive in the changing room. All of that, and we are about to lose it, and we are going to lose it to Manchester United. It was like your worst nightmare. And to be losing that football match, no disrespect to QPR, but the fact that Mark Hughes was the Manager of QPR, it was like, 'This is retribution day.'"

Al Mubarak is convinced that the nervous energy in the stands had an impact on events on the pitch that day.

"The spillover was heavy," he says. "It's almost like people didn't believe that this team could succeed. It was like a conviction that something bad was going to happen. Even when something good is happening, something's going to screw it up at the end. Many fans felt that way. Not all of them, but many fans felt that way. And to be honest, it spills over on the team. And then just to confirm that, you're playing at home, you're playing against a team that's fighting relegation, all we need to do is win and you're the Premier League champions. And then, we're down 2-1 in the 90th minute."

"You're going to get me started on a topic here," says Kompany, when asked about the impact a crowd's energy can have on the players on the pitch, "but it's crucial, you know. I don't know how much I want to go into the science here, but there's actually studies that have been done that link atmosphere to testosterone levels, and to increased behaviour of territoriality in players. So, for me it's really important. I think that good atmosphere helps players sharpen up and stay focused. I really believe it. It's the difference between a one all draw or winning two-, three-, four-nil. It just pushes you on."

The crowd and the players would soon get the push they so desperately needed, when substitute Edin Džeko rose up and tied the game with a better-late-than-never goal in the 92nd minute. As the powerful header ballooned off the back of the net, Sergio Agüero caught the ball before it had even hit the ground, and raced back to halfway to restart the game. Less than three minutes later, he would be buried under a mass of bodies after scoring the match-winning goal in the 94th minute.

With two improbable goals in added time, Manchester City had won 3-2 and were officially Premier League champions. For a few uncertain moments, after they'd beaten Sunderland but before Agüero had scored, Manchester United's players had every reason to believe that they had just won the League.

"The afternoon of Sunday 13 May 2012 was crushing," Sir Alex Ferguson would later write in his autobiography. "Of all the setbacks I endured, nothing compared to losing the League to City."[14]

"It was such an unexpected triumph," says John MacBeath, then interim CEO, "because I defy any Manchester City fan to say that at eighty-nine-and-a-half minutes, they thought that outcome was a possibility. We were there in hope, because you always hope in football, and it came to pass. Unbelievable. If you wrote it as a script it would be torn up as being too fantastic."

"Even watching it now I start crying," says Mike Summerbee, who had played for Manchester City the last time the Club had won the League in 1967-68 [also won on the last day of the season and ending with Manchester United in second place]. "It's not easy to talk about, but it's something that will stay in my mind for the rest of my life. I've never seen a moment in football like that, and a lot of people who were watching the game will never see a moment like that again."

"I think that win, in that way, created folklore," says Al Mubarak. "Not just winning the League, but winning it that way, will never be forgotten. Not just by Manchester City fans, but by most football fans. I mean, this is almost unprecedented in sports. Winning the League that way will be a defining moment in the Club's history forever. It also gave us this global arrival in a way that I think has also served us very well. And you know, we wouldn't have had that. The arrival would have been different. So, I look back, and if you ask me, 'If you could play it back again, would you have wanted that game finished 2-0 or 3-0 in the first half, and then you breeze through the second half and win the League that way, or this way?'"

Al Mubarak doesn't hesitate.

"This way, a hundred per cent."

Six years later, Kompany remains perplexed by two odd conversations he had with teammates in the lead-up to those final two games.

"We went to Newcastle for the second-last game of the season," recalls Kompany, "and Yaya [Touré] came up to me in the hotel and he said, 'Oh Vinnie. You know, you've headed the ball and tackled brilliantly all season. Thank you. Now,' and he taps his chest, 'leave it to me.' I was like, 'What is he on about? Oh, Yaya being himself again.' So, I just go and do my thing. Next thing you know, we play this game, win 2-0, and Yaya scores two goals. You know, big players, big moments kind of thing. Then, we prepare for the QPR game, and Kun [Agüero] does the same thing. He comes to me and says, 'Vinnie, today, leave it to me.' You know, they'd never done this before. They'd never done it before, they've never done it after. Only these two games. I'll remember it forever."

For the majority of the QPR game, Agüero's confidence had seemed misplaced.

"And Kun plays this game," recalls Kompany, "and after the first half I knew he wasn't in it. Like, he was really poor."

Agüero doesn't disagree.

"I couldn't escape the fact that I was playing like a dog and nothing was going for me," he later wrote about the match in the introduction to his 2014 book, 'Born to Rise.' "In fact, everything I tried failed. Of all the games to play as though I had two left feet!"[5]

"And I'm like, 'Oh, he's full of [expletive]. What a load of rubbish,'" says Kompany. "And second half I'm getting even more angry, because I'm like, 'He's come and given me the big talk, and now we're going to lose this thing.' Obviously, there's no blame on him, but I was just thinking, 'Why would you come and say that? Why did you jinx it?' And then last minute, last second, as if it was a prophesy, he just turns up and scores this goal, on a pass which was the only assist that Mario Balotelli ever had at Manchester City, and I'm thinking, 'How did they do it?'"

Kompany laughs as he reflects on that incredible moment.

"How did they do it?"

CHAPTER 11:

THE TOLL

The 2011-12 premiership was Manchester City's first League title since 1968. It was the closest title race in Premier League history and the first to be settled on goal difference. The breaking of Manchester United's heart in the process only made the moment sweeter for many Manchester City supporters. However, before the pain had subsided on the first of the "93:20" tattoos applied across Greater Manchester that evening, the attention of key figures inside the Club had already turned to what would come next.

"You celebrate, but you don't celebrate," says Brian Marwood, recalling the night that Manchester City became the champions of England. "I was just too tired. I remember sitting in a chair with my wife, and I just sat there with a glass in my hand. I was just drained. I was completely and utterly drained."

For many employees of Manchester City, the win was a spectacular reward for years of hard work and sacrifice. Not all of it had been easy or pleasant though, and the process had left some scars.

"It wasn't about that day for me," explains Marwood. "It was about starting this job in 2009. It was about all of the changes. It was about the firing of people. It was about the hiring of people. It was about protecting good people. It was about the methodology that we had wanted to create. It was about getting the business side right. It was about getting the players in. It was about a hundred things, and all of it led to that moment in time, and it was surreal. Did I enjoy it? Yes, of course, we won the League, but I was just so drained. And then you're thinking, 'We've got to go and win another one, and another one, and it's always going to be like this, and I am not sure I can keep going through this.' For many people, it was a strange day."

One of those people was former CEO, Garry Cook, who attended the match [his first since his resignation seven months earlier], but couldn't bring himself to make an appearance at the Club's post-match function later that evening.

"I went to a couple of bars for a few drinks," says Cook, who slipped out of one venue after a group of well-meaning patrons recognised him and began singing his name. "There was a party back at the Lowry. They [his former colleagues at Manchester City] had invited me back, and I was going to go, but I just did not get there in the end. I just got in a taxi and went home. So, I never really got to celebrate, which was a shame really. I just felt really weird. I felt awkward. I just did not handle it very well, I suppose."

Cook says he found the whole day to be a bittersweet experience; a historic day for Manchester City and the Premier League, but a gut-wrenching reminder of just how much he missed it all.

"I was there," he says, "and I got to witness one of the greatest moments in football history, and everybody remembers it with great joy and pride. It was unbelievable. But I had a very different view, a mixture of both love and despair, and that is why I went home that night. I just could not cope. It was an awful lot for me to think that I had walked away from that."

"We were all knackered," says board member Simon Pearce, summing up the general feeling around the Club at that time. "We were tired, but we weren't just tired from that one season. We were tired from all of the seasons that had got us to that point. We had lost Garry [Cook], and John was doing the job that was asked of him very well, but the Club required a new injection of energy at that time, and John wasn't in a position to do that, because his mandate was temporary. We were all absolutely shattered, and you know what the realisation was? We've got to do it again, and actually you have got to do it again, and again, and again, and get used to it, because this is every year now."

Even Sir Alex Ferguson, the veteran Manager of Manchester United, was left questioning his desire to continue for much longer at the end of that dramatic season, later writing in his autobiography that after that exhausting final day, he already knew his next season would probably be his last.[16]

However, respite would be in short supply. Within months, Manchester City and Manchester United would be at it again, this time competing for the services of Arsenal striker Robin Van Persie.

"We wanted Robin that summer, and Roberto [Mancini] wanted Robin," admits Marwood, who led the unsuccessful bid for the Dutch striker. "At the beginning of the summer we were in a really good place, but I think we had something like seven or eight strikers at the time that were all earning very good money. Khaldoon [Al Mubarak] was worried about that, and Financial Fair Play was coming down the road as well. The message was 'Yeah, we want Robin, but you need to sell some players,' and of course we had been a buying club and not necessarily a selling club, and because these players were all on astronomical salaries, there weren't many other clubs that could afford them. That created a delay in the exiting of players, and that allowed Manchester United to come in and say to Robin, 'Listen, you are going to play, you are going to be there with Rooney, and it's going to be you two,' and he was looking at Man City and going, 'Well, they've got eight strikers, so where do I fit in with all of those?'"

The state of the Club's finances also weighed on the decision. Although Manchester City had stemmed the bleeding and halved its losses in 2011-12 on a year-by-year basis, it had still reported an annual loss of £97.9m.

"We were trying to balance all of that," explains Marwood, who took some hits during this period from both inside and outside the Club. "Do we want that type of player? Absolutely. But at any cost? Well, no. We had a lot of work to do, and we lost Robin, and of course I was public enemy number one and in the firing line again, but you accept it."

"So, this was the problem of storming the top table," says Pearce. "We had to pay people more money than they were going to get elsewhere. Then we had to get our wage bill right down, and at that time it was almost 100 per cent of our revenue. We are now [in 2018] down at 55 per cent, which is a healthy place to be. That was the first sign of the inhibitors coming into play. That was it, and United got to go and get Van Persie."

Throughout the process, Manager Roberto Mancini made no secret of his frustration with the Club's inactivity in the transfer market, and who he held personally responsible.

"For this question, speak to the man in charge," he told reporters while the team was on tour in China in July 2012, adding that "We have a man [Marwood] who works for this, and we hope that they can do a good job."

A month later, when the battle for Van Persie was all but lost, and a week before the prized striker signed with Manchester United, an exasperated Mancini continued to air the Club's dirty laundry in public.

"These questions you should ask other people," he told the media in August 2012, when asked about potential player signings. "I don't know what I can say. After three or four months, nothing."

He then proceeded to swat away further questions about the Club's transfer policy, noting: "You should talk to Brian Marwood for this. Not me. Talk to Marwood please."

The public campaign took a toll on Marwood, and in late 2012, he requested a face-to-face meeting with the Chairman, Khaldoon Al Mubarak, to discuss his future at the Club.

"It got to the point where I just thought, 'This is not worth it. I'm not prepared to put myself or my family through this,'" he says.

The two soon met over breakfast in the Chairman's suite at Manchester's Lowry hotel, just six floors up from where they had celebrated the Club's maiden Premier League title only three months earlier.

This was a less happy occasion.

"I said, 'Khaldoon, I am going to make this easy for you,'" recalls Marwood. "I said, 'You know how these things work. I can't do this anymore. I don't want you to have a difficult situation, so I'm going to resign,' and he just said, 'Let me stop you there. You're not going anywhere.'"

"He was going through a very rough time," says Al Mubarak, who remembers the conversation well. "I think there were many items that Brian fundamentally disagreed with Roberto about, but he had just won the League, and most of these things, the whole world didn't know. It was a difficult time, but I had to assure him that at the end of the day, there are people within any football club that become part of the DNA of that organisation, and that have to stay with that organisation, because they are the people that will carry out its vision and really sustain it. And then there are people that come in and out."

Al Mubarak says it isn't about playing favourites. It's about understanding the nature of people's roles.

"Roberto fell directly into the category of people that will come in and out," he says. "Whether he stayed a year, two, three or four, in his capacity he was always going to be someone that would come, do a job, but ultimately it was not going to last. Brian, on the other hand, fell right dead bang into that first category of individuals that has to be part of the long-term DNA of this project. So, I had to tell him that, 'Listen, we are in a period of heavy turbulence, but you just need to weather the storm. We have to work together to deal with it, but you have to weather it.'"

Roberto Mancini would leave Manchester City nine months later. Despite finishing second in both the Premier League and FA Cup in 2012-13, the Club reported that it had failed to meet its football targets for the season, with the exception of qualifying for the UEFA Champions League.

"The one campaign that I think we should have won and didn't win, was that second year [2012-13]," maintains Al Mubarak. "The reality is that we were the best team by a mile that season, and we should have won the League comfortably. But we didn't win it. We had the best team in the League, but I think we screwed it up."

The Chairman met Mancini in London the day after the FA Cup final loss on 11 May 2013 to break the news in person. They met privately in the Chairman's suite at the Mandarin Oriental hotel, upstairs from where they had celebrated the Club's FA Cup triumph two years earlier. Mancini was ousted ten months into a new five-year contract, and two games before the end of the season.

"Khaldoon left it entirely in his hands," says Pearce. "Do you want to coach through to the end of the year, or do you want to go now? The recommendation was to go now. Get it done clean, go now, and we are not going to have you standing in the rain on Tuesday [coaching away at Reading]. You know, Roberto has such a sense of honour, he didn't want to walk away, even though it would have done him harm to stay. He was like 'No, I'll see this through to the end. I don't care about the humiliation.' But it was just unnecessary. It didn't need to be that way."

Mancini decided to go immediately. He then put a full-page advertisement in the Manchester Evening News. It thanked the Manchester City fans for three unforgettable years, told them they would always be in his heart, and signed off in Italian, "Ciao." Displayed prominently in the foreground of the ad, partially obscuring a scarfed Mancini, stood a glistening FA Cup [won 2010-11], Premier League trophy [won 2011-12], and Community Shield [won 2012-13], leaving a message that required no translation. Ten days later, a group of Manchester City fans returned the favour, placing an advertisement thanking Mancini in the Italian newspaper, La Gazetta dello Sport.

"We used to speak, me and Mancini, almost every day," says Al Mubarak, reflecting on his close relationship with the Manager. "Many times I would come before games, and we used to organise a football game, and we'd play on the same team. We had a unique relationship, but ultimately, we had to part ways, and that was a very difficult period. He didn't take it too well. That was not a pleasant period of time, and you'd like for these relationships and these friendships to remain, and to withstand professional differences. Unfortunately, with Mancini, he took it very personally, and we didn't speak for years."

Al Mubarak says the two have since reconciled.

"The year after has always been a bit of a let-down," says Vincent Kompany, when asked about the Club's failed attempt to defend its Premier League title in 2012-13, "and I can't really say that it's just been at City. I won two titles with Anderlecht in Belgium and it's always been the same story. The year after has always been difficult for whatever reason."

"It's something in the eyes," explains Kompany. "You see it in pre-season. You're a little bit more relaxed, a little bit more happy and comfortable with yourself. And before you know it, you lose grip, and you think 'Okay, I'm going to recover it, I'm going to recover it,' but you don't recover it. So, whatever you have, it can be momentum, it can be luck, but anything you have, you have to hold on to it as much as you can, and not let it go under any circumstances. Whether you were champions ten games before the end of the season, or you go back into a new pre-season after winning everything, you can't let it go, because it's so hard to recover."

Txiki Begiristain, who won four La Liga titles as a player and another four as Football Director at FC Barcelona, before being hired by Manchester City's new CEO, Ferran

Soriano [who joined in August 2012], to be the Club's new Football Director in November 2012, agrees.

"It happens to everybody," says Begiristain. "Not only the players, but everybody in the organisation. The problem is that you think that you are doing the same things, but you aren't. You are convinced that you are training the same way. So, the players think, 'No, I am training the same way. I am okay. I am the same guy,' but they are not the same guy. It only takes two per cent, three per cent, or five per cent less intensity in training, and in this League, that is the difference between being champions, or being fifth or sixth."

Manchester United were crowned Premier League champions on 22 April 2013. Robin Van Persie won the Golden Boot with 26 goals, including a 90th minute winner in his first ever Manchester derby in December 2012. Manchester United finished the season with 89 points [the same number of points that had seen them beaten by Manchester City on goal difference in 2011-12]. By contrast, Manchester City finished with 78. It was Manchester United's 13th Premier League title under Sir Alex Ferguson who retired at the end of the season.

"We had turned the tables on City," Ferguson later wrote in his autobiography of his Premier League swansong in 2012-13. "But I would not be taking them on again."[17]

THE CREATION OF CITY FOOTBALL GROUP

CHAPTER 12:

CITY NEVER SLEEPS

When Garry Cook resigned from Manchester City in September 2011, Chairman Khaldoon Al Mubarak instructed board directors, Simon Pearce and Marty Edelman, to immediately commence a global search for a new CEO.

It took them less than three months to settle on a standout candidate in the form of Ferran Soriano, a Catalan businessman who had previously served as Vice President and General Manager of FC Barcelona. At their recommendation, a one-on-one meeting was soon set up between Soriano and Al Mubarak in late 2011.

It was one of those meetings that was meant to be about one thing but quickly became about something else. During their conversation, Soriano explained that back in 2005, while he was heading FC Barcelona, the Club had explored the idea of establishing an affiliated Major League Soccer [MLS] team in the US. They had discussed the concept with MLS Commissioner, Don Garber, but it had never really got off the ground. Soriano had shared the same anecdote with Pearce and Edelman in their earlier interviews.

"When he said that," recalls Al Mubarak, "it actually immediately clicked with me, and I started probing it further."

The main thing the Manchester City Chairman wondered, was: "Why?"

"He said literally," remembers Soriano, "I am intrigued by this."

Soriano and Al Mubarak then discussed how it could be done, including speaking about the concept of a hypothetical "football group" that owned multiple clubs around the world, and the benefits that such an approach could potentially deliver to Manchester City.

By the end of that meeting, Al Mubarak says that he had reached two conclusions. One, Manchester City had found its new CEO. And two, he was convinced that for Manchester City to succeed, it had to do something different.

"We couldn't just keep following that one dimensional, conventional way of building the Club," he says. "We had to do something different, and the idea of actually having multiple clubs around the world, the idea of 'City' branding, and having, let's say a team in the United States, a team somewhere else. I mean, we didn't even know where we were going to go. But that idea made sense, and I left the meeting saying, 'Ferran, think about this. We're going to make you an offer, but also, I want you to evolve that thought into something more.'"

Although the idea of a professional club putting a team in a foreign league wasn't unheard of at the time – as Soriano noted in his 2011 book, 'Goal: The Ball Doesn't Go In By Chance,' Ajax Amsterdam and Chivas de Guadalajara had established satellites in South Africa and the US respectively – it was still a high-risk exercise.[18] In an ideal world, Manchester City executives would have spent at least 6-12 months plotting out an international expansion strategy and gearing up internally to execute such a challenging project.

As it turned out, this was a luxury they wouldn't have. After agreeing to join Manchester City, but before officially putting his feet under the desk in August 2012, Soriano called MLS Commissioner Don Garber to confirm that the New York franchise they had discussed years earlier – and that Soriano had been touting to his new employers – was indeed still available. The answer was 'Yes, but not for long.' MLS had interest from a rival party that was believed to have the money to make it happen. The New York Times would later report that up to six potential investors had enquired about the franchise.[19]

"So, then I spoke to Marty Edelman, to Khaldoon, and I said to them, 'If we want to do this, we need to rush,'" recalls Soriano.

"Ferran started," recalls Edelman, "and the first thing he said was, 'We need to go to New York, because there is an open franchise in New York City.' I said, 'Well, that didn't take long, right?'"

So, on only his second day on the job, the long-awaited new CEO of Manchester City wasn't in the City of Manchester at all. He was walking down Fifth Avenue with Marty Edelman, on their way to MLS headquarters to express Manchester City's interest in establishing a professional soccer team in New York City.

MLS explained to them that the price tag on the New York City franchise had been set at US$100m. That was just for the licence too. It wouldn't cover the cost of creating a new club from scratch – including building a soccer-specific stadium – in one of the most densely-populated and expensive cities in the world. Before recommending the proposal to owner Sheikh Mansour, Al Mubarak wanted to see the business case for making such a significant investment outside of the UK.

"I think Marty was the first to be convinced," says Soriano, "I spent time in New York with him, and after talking to people, I think he embraced the idea quickly. Khaldoon also embraced the idea, but he was waiting for us to deliver a business plan that made sense."

In November 2012, Soriano tapped Don Dransfield, then Head of Strategy and Business Planning at Manchester City FC, and Francisco Lopez, a former finance director at FC Barcelona, to develop the business case for New York City FC. The starting point was a financial model for the new franchise that had been prepared in advance by MLS and its advisors. However, it wasn't easy to make reliable financial projections for a club that didn't exist yet.

"Most football clubs in the UK have existed for a long time," explains Dransfield, "and therefore have years of history, both with regards to ticketing and commercial revenues, and a lot of those things can be forecast moving forward, because sales and partnership contracts typically last for three to six years. So, there's a certain amount of revenue, and certain amount of cost, that you can assume with certainty."

That wasn't the case in New York City.

"This was completely new," says Dransfield, "because there were no fans, there were no commercial deals, there were no costs, there were no players. There was nothing. So, we were building from scratch all of the assumptions, based only on the benchmark figures that had been provided to us, and the modelling that Major League Soccer had done."

"After a few months," recalls Soriano, "we had a detailed presentation about the opportunity in New York that we took Khaldoon through."

Satisfied with the proposal, the Chairman presented the opportunity to Sheikh Mansour.

"The big thesis," explains Al Mubarak, "was how do we give the Group, and Manchester City as part of the Group, a commercial advantage? We were investing, from day one of the purchase of the Club, to build a team that could compete. And sure enough, by 2012 we got there. We won the League. But now, we knew that the daunting task was the next one, which was, how do we distinguish ourselves commercially? Is having a team in MLS, and having teams in Asia, going to give us an edge when we go talk to Nissan, or Cisco, or Amazon, or any of these global sponsors? Because if we just go head-to-head, it's not an easy sell. The thesis was, if we go with a global proposition, that could give us the edge."

It therefore came as no surprise to Al Mubarak when the entrepreneurial Sheikh Mansour gave his Chairman the green light to pursue the New York franchise.

"He came back and said, 'We're okay, let's do it,'" recalls Soriano, who knew those few words marked the beginning of a very long road.

"Then there's the process of negotiating the deal and creating the start-up," he explains. "The whole new world starts."

It was at this point that CFG began to explore the concept of bringing a local partner on board to help execute the project.

"New York is a very challenging, big city," explains Al Mubarak, who has overseen a number of high-profile projects in the US during his career in business and government, "and to be working and investing in New York without a partner, right off the bat, we knew that would be a big mistake."

However, who that partner should be was an open question.

"In selecting a local partner," explains Edelman, "we had a lot of choices. You can just get investors, politically-connected people, or people in another sport. And through a series of lucky breaks we were able to talk to the New York Yankees, who are an amazing international brand."

"The idea was basically to partner with somebody who had an anchor here in New York," says Randy Levine, President of the New York Yankees, "and the Yankees have a long history of being successful here in New York, as one of the premier, if not the premier, sports franchises in the world."

Following an initial phone call between Edelman and Levine, a face-to-face meeting was set up to discuss the opportunity in more detail and to consider what each side could bring to the table.

"Marty and I met," recalls Levine, "and it took us not a long a time at all to talk about the parameters of what the agreement would be. We came to a fairly quick agreement. Marty introduced me to Ferran and Khaldoon Al Mubarak. I brought [Yankees' Managing General Partner] Hal Steinbrenner and our Group into it, and you know, Hal Steinbrenner is a big soccer fan. Very knowledgeable. So, it just made sense to do. That's how it came about."

According to Levine, the partnership was a natural fit for the Yankees' ownership.

"Yankee Global Enterprises, which predominantly owns the Yankees, is a sports and entertainment company," says Levine. "We have great partnerships with great people all over. So, the idea of partnering with Manchester City was very appealing to us, because they're the type of world-class partner that we have partnered with and been very successful. We thought soccer, and MLS in particular, was something that was on the upswing and that would grow. And we liked the people."

For CFG, the Yankees were an ideal partner for a number of reasons.

"Having the Yankees as a minority partner," explains Edelman, "where they don't interfere with the football, which they've been terrific about, gave us two things. First, they gave us an iconic stadium [allowing New York City FC to play home games at Yankee Stadium on an interim basis], and they validated us in a way."

It is telling that even one of the world's biggest football clubs felt the need for validation in New York City.

"So here we are," explains Edelman, "a bunch of guys from Manchester City, and when you look behind Manchester City there's this foreign owner that people don't know a lot about, and the Yankees helped us a lot with that."

Pearce concurs that the presence of the Yankees added value from a branding perspective.

"I think getting the Yankees on board was massive," he says, "because it meant we had New York in our DNA."

According to CFG officials, Yankee Global Enterprises has also brought a wealth of commercial intelligence and local sports industry expertise to the partnership.

"They've been very helpful," says Edelman. "They help us with the press, they help us with their insights into the way sports are run in New York, and they were really helpful to us in our first TV contract. And of course, they invested in us. They paid for a piece of the team. It's not like we gave it to them because they are the Yankees."

Meanwhile, blueprints for the CFG superstructure required to own and operate multiple clubs on separate continents had been steadily taking shape behind the scenes. Since the summer of 2012, Soriano and Pearce had been quietly trading drafts on an evolving document that would become known internally as the CFG White Paper.

This confidential memo mapped out a proposed corporate structure for CFG that would allow each of its clubs to operate independently while seamlessly drawing on the vast technical and commercial know-how that had been built up in Manchester. At its core, that meant creating two new in-house service companies – City Football Services [now called Global Football] and City Football Marketing – that were equipped to provide bespoke football and commercial services to CFG clubs around the world, and potentially others outside of the Group.

Written in 2012, while Manchester City was the only 'City club,' the document imagined a future in which there would be several clubs in the CFG orbit, competing in different leagues around the world, all playing a consistent and attractive style of football, with players potentially moving between clubs to suit different stages of their careers. Many of these things have since transpired.

As the race for the New York City franchise was ramping up, the CFG White Paper left no doubt about its strategic importance to the broader vision: "The process starts with the purchase of the New York MLS franchise in 2012, and its subsequent branding as New York "City" Football Club [NYCFC]."

CHAPTER 13:

A SECOND CHANCE TO MAKE A FIRST IMPRESSION

When the time came to go public with plans for the creation of New York City FC in May 2013, the deadline day circus of 1 September 2008 loomed large in the memory of Manchester City and ADUG officials. Four years later, there was zero appetite for repeating the exercise in New York City. How the new MLS club was introduced to the world, and how its officials conducted themselves, would all set an indelible tone that would stay with the organisation for years to come.

With that in mind, in early 2013, CFG tapped strategic market research firm Edelman Berland [now Edelman Intelligence] to conduct a wide-ranging analysis of attitudes to sport, soccer and MLS among over a thousand respondents from the New York area. That research produced a number of important findings.

First, awareness of MLS was low in New York City and the competition was viewed by many as "a start-up league and only somewhat capable of being ready for a world-class team."

Second, the combined ownership of Manchester City FC and the New York Yankees [who would own a minority stake in the team under the deal struck between CFG and Yankee Global Enterprises] would set high expectations for the new franchise both on and off the pitch, with respondents reporting that "the team needs to be as successful as (it is) stylish, as authentic New York as (it is) European world-class, and a genuine member of the NYC community."

Third, New York City FC would be expected to walk the fine line between confidence and arrogance, with respondents – unimpressed by bullish test messages boasting that the new team would "dominate" the League – offering the researchers some friendly advice on behalf of the people of New York City: "You have to earn it before you can say it, and once you get to that stage, it goes without saying for a NYC team."

However, New York City FC would be more than just a New York City team. It would also be part of CFG. In fact, as the first 'City club' outside of Manchester, New York City FC would be the lens through which most people would come to learn about the unconventional CFG model.

CFG CEO, Ferran Soriano, is evangelical about how these two strands of DNA are intended to fit together.

"New York City FC is a New York team," he says emphatically. "It's not Manchester City. It's a real, authentic team with its roots in New York. However, the technical football engine that lies behind it has been engineered in Europe, because that is where the best soccer is played. And we will help them, because we will provide the resources, and we will provide the technical knowledge, but they will shape their own identity. Like it has happened with FC Barcelona, Real Madrid, all the big teams in the world that are in big cities. They are part of the fabric of the city, and they evolve with the history and people of the city. And there's nothing commercial about this. It's not a marketing trick. It's all identity and emotion."

This founding principle – that being a 'New York team' and a 'City team' need not be mutually-exclusive – has infused every aspect of the Club's roll-out.

"The best way to understand what we're doing," explains Tom Glick, Chief Commercial Officer of CFG and former President of New York City FC, "and how we still look at New York, is that we are a group of local clubs, with their own local identities. And then we look for synergies that can add value. But at the end of the day, the idea of New York was always to create a club for New York, not a Manchester City in New York. We didn't want to impose anything other than the fact that we were sure we wanted to call it 'City' and we wanted to play in light blue on home games. Everything else was really built with the idea that this is going to be New York's club."

There is also an undeniable commercial logic to the team putting its roots down firmly in New York City.

"Owning the brand 'New York City' for soccer is a huge asset," says Soriano. "We don't know whether it's an asset in the next 10 years, or the next 150 years, but I am sure. I won't be here, you won't be here, but in 150 years, owning the soccer brand of New York City is a big asset."

Soriano is quick to clarify that New York City already boasted high levels of passion for the sport. In fact, there was already one MLS team servicing the New York metropolitan area, in the form of the New York Red Bulls, even though its home ground and training facility are in New Jersey.

"We didn't go to New York and tell New Yorkers, 'This is soccer, you've got to love it,'" says Soriano. "Soccer existed in New York. Soccer was already very present in the city. There's a million people in New York City who love soccer. We just gave them a platform for soccer to flourish, because we provided the resources, and the organisation, and the brand – the obvious brand, New York City FC – to allow soccer fans in New York to galvanise, to get together, and to grow."

"New York has tons of informed and passionate soccer fans," agrees Glick, "and they were following soccer in many other ways before our team arrived, and in one respect we were just the lucky ones who got a chance to bring a professional team to the five boroughs. Because they were certainly ready for it. These fans were ready for it."

However, you can't manufacture a relationship with a city. And long before it had thought about investing in a MLS franchise, Manchester City had begun establishing its own presence in New York City. On a pre-season tour back in 2010, the Club had announced the donation of a rooftop football pitch to P.S. 72 [Lexington Academy] in East Harlem. Completed in 2012, the blue rooftop pitch is still visible from planes on their descent into LaGuardia Airport.

In May 2013, things came full circle when P.S. 72 was chosen as the venue to announce the establishment of New York City FC to the world, as part of Manchester City's post-season tour of the US. In a packed press conference convened in the school's humble cafeteria, Soriano was joined on-stage by New York City Mayor Michael Bloomberg, MLS Commissioner Don Garber, Managing General Partner of the New York Yankees, Hal Steinbrenner, President of the New York Yankees, Randy Levine, and former Manchester City player and Sporting Director of New York City FC, Claudio Reyna, for the high-profile announcement.

"I think when we held the press conference to announce the fact that we had become owners of the franchise, and it was at P.S. 72, that was incredibly important," says CFG board member, Simon Pearce, "because we could only go there because we'd done the right thing by New York before. And three years later, after the arduous journey of trying to get this pitch built on the roof, we turned up at this school and the Principal [Tony Hernandez] spoke about how we were the right organisation for New York, you know, with tears in his eyes, absolutely committed to it. For me, that was the biggest moment."

Kloss, who ranks the donation of the rooftop pitch at P.S. 72 as one of the high points of her 17 years with Manchester City, agrees it was a powerful statement.

"Nothing made my soul sing more than the fact that we were able to do it there," she says, "based on something that was so real and had pre-dated this announcement. Three years earlier, we had delivered a pitch to these kids who wouldn't otherwise have been able to find a place to play. I know it's a tiny little thing, in an enormous landscape, but we'd done something real, and brought our Manchester community spirit into this pocket of New York. Then we were able to revisit that, and it gave us a platform, and it felt good. It felt like we weren't just some fly-by-nights that had rocked up and said, 'Hey, we're going to take on New York.'"

Not everything went to plan that day. Noticeably absent for the first part of the ceremony was the touring Manchester City squad. It was only midway through the opening speeches when a sheepish Vincent Kompany led his team mates into the crowded cafeteria. In what everybody hoped was a coincidence, rather than an omen, the Manchester City bus had taken a wrong turn on the way to the press conference, and the team had got lost in New York.

CHAPTER 14:

THE FIRST HIRES

Claudio Reyna played 87 games for Manchester City between 2003 and 2007. Six years later, he would reconnect with his former club as the new Sporting Director – and first employee – of New York City FC.

"Having previously played at Manchester City," remembers Reyna, who also captained the US national team at the 2006 World Cup, "I always stayed in touch with the Club. As I was keeping in touch, there were so many changes, the big one being the takeover by Sheikh Mansour. Having been at Manchester City prior to the takeover, and prior to the previous owners, I was there and I say this respectfully, but it was a completely different club in a matter of four years."

On a visit to Manchester in late 2012, Reyna met Brian Marwood, Manchester City's former Chief Football Administration Officer, who was in the process of setting up CFG's new City Football Services arm [now known as Global Football]. What Reyna didn't know at the time was that Marwood was on the lookout for somebody that could head up football operations for a new MLS franchise in New York City.

"It's a big job, right?" says Marwood, of the first position that he had to fill at New York City FC. "I mean, the beauty of the Group is that we have an organisation that can help and support the other clubs, so I knew that I had a group of people that could support the building of the football operation, but at the same time, I needed to be able to trust somebody that was on the ground, seven days a week, twenty-four-seven, just really focused on doing the right thing."

As a New Yorker, former Manchester City player, former US team captain, and the current Technical Director of US Soccer, Reyna ticked a lot of boxes.

"Nothing was mentioned then [about CFG establishing a team in the US]," recalls Reyna of that meeting, "but I remember Brian, in particular, asking me questions about MLS, and about the future of soccer in the States, and my thoughts, having been born there, and having been through the whole system."

"It was his unofficial interview, really," admits Marwood. "One of my greatest advisors in life is 'Mister Gut Feeling,' and he just seemed such a good fit. Like any of these things, you consider a number of people, you meet a number of people, you speak to a number of people, but when I met him, and we didn't really know each other before then, it just felt right from day one."

As it turned out, Mister Gut Feeling wasn't Reyna's only character reference on the Etihad Campus that day. Vicky Kloss, now Chief Communications Officer for CFG, had worked with Reyna as a player when he had joined Manchester City in 2003.

"He just was an ultimate pro," says Kloss of Reyna in his playing days. "Like Frank Lampard is. Like Patrick Vieira is. That was Claudio. Totally understood his responsibilities as a footballer, off the pitch as well as on it. He was the type of player that when you go to him and say, 'Can you help me with this interview?', he always said 'Yes.' And sometimes you might be in a difficult situation, where the team might have played terribly. They've been absolutely battered. No player wants to do media after the game. Claudio was always the guy that would do it."

"I spoke to Vicky about it," says Marwood, "and she went 'Yeah, absolutely. Really good guy, somebody that's very trustworthy, somebody that's very serious about his football, very articulate.' Plus, he was working for US Soccer at that time, so he was ingrained in the business side of football. He just felt like a really strong fit for us."

"I said, 'Look, I can't vouch for his coaching abilities or whatever," remembers Kloss, "but I can vouch for the fact that he is a thinker. He's definitely smart, has huge respect from those around him, and I can't believe he's gone backwards from the time that I knew him. And he's also got City in his blood, right? He understands City.

So, on paper, without knowing what his coaching and business credentials are, he'd be perfect.'"

After returning to the US, Reyna soon got an inkling why American soccer had been on Marwood's mind.

"A couple of months later, not even that," he remembers, "something leaked here about it. And it was, you know, Manchester City was going to buy a club in New York City."

The timing was fortuitous. After three years as the Technical Director for US Soccer, Reyna was already planning a move back into the professional game. He soon learned that CFG had earmarked him as part of its plans for New York City FC. It was too early to put an offer on the table, but he was urged not to sign with anybody else. Enticed by the chance to help build something from the ground up, Reyna passed up at least two offers from professional teams in Europe and the US as he waited for his former club to put something in writing.

"For me, it was just amazing to see the Club and the direction it was going," explains Reyna. "I mean, having been a former player there, I just had an interest and a real desire to be a part of it."

Reyna's patience was rewarded in February 2013, when he returned to Manchester for face-to-face interviews with Soriano and Al Mubarak, and was subsequently offered the job as New York City FC's first Sporting Director.

"Everybody thought about Claudio because he had played at Manchester City, he was a figure in US soccer, and because he had been in Manchester recently," explains Soriano, "so he was the one that was charged with starting to think about the football side of things. He was actually the first real, permanent employee. Everybody else had been sent temporarily from other places."

"Isn't it funny?" says Vicky Kloss, on Reyna's return to the City fold. "When something is right, it's just right, and you could not have written a more perfect person to fulfill the job spec. He just had all the attributes, and also for New York, not only was he massively respected through a UK lens, but he'd done it at the highest level in Europe, which was a relatively rare thing for a US footballer."

Reyna's appointment was announced at New York City FC's inaugural press conference in May 2013. Although it had the backing of two of the biggest names in professional sports – Manchester City and the New York Yankees – at that point, the new franchise largely existed in name only. Without office space of its own, Reyna, Dransfield and Lopez, early hires Christina Hawkins and Janine Padilla, and a fly-in-fly-out Soriano, annexed a handful of desks at MLS offices to serve as the start-up Club's temporary HQ. Tim Pernetti, formerly Director of Athletics at Rutgers University, joined soon after as New York City FC's first Chief Business Officer in September 2013.

"Ferran had to create, not just a football organisation, but a business organisation," explains CFG board member and Vice Chairman of New York City FC, Marty Edelman. "And Manchester City has enormously talented people, but you couldn't just put them all here in New York, for a lot of reasons. One, we needed them in Manchester, and two, you can't just transplant things to another place. You have to have some homegrown product."

"This was a new club," says Marwood. "It didn't have a stadium, didn't have a training ground, didn't have people. It had a group of people in Manchester that was led by me, that then went and recruited a Sporting Director, which was Claudio, and then it was like, 'Right, okay, what's the vision? What's the strategic direction for the next 3-5 years? What's the budget? What can we spend on players? What can we spend on infrastructure? What can we spend on getting the right people? Where do we need to prioritise? And then how do we build from there?'"

"For me," remembers Reyna, "the first thing was, 'Where are we going to train?'. We had to get up and running in 18 months and we had no facility. Then after that, it was coaches and players. The expansion draft was coming up. How were we going to approach that? Assistant coaches. Medical team. Everything. Every single staff member had to be hired."

Arguably the most important position that had to be filled was that of Head Coach, with the Club appointing the former MLS and US national team player, and Real Salt Lake coach, Jason Kreis, to be its first ever Manager in January 2014.

"I think for me it was very, very important to have someone with knowledge of the League," said Reyna at Kreis's unveiling. "The teams he'll be coaching against. The players we're going to be playing and competing against. The ones we'll be potentially taking in the expansion draft. So, it was always important for me to have, first, an American coach, but [also] an American coach specifically who had a tremendous amount of knowledge of the League, and Jason ticked all the boxes."

Kreis spoke openly that day about the pressures that would come with the position.

"Of course, the expectations are there, and the challenges will be there, and the pressures are all going to be there," he said. "We know that we're expected to win, and frankly, we will win. So, it's not something that I've shied away from, it's not something that I'm nervous about. It is what it is. And to be frank with you, anybody that knows me, I'm sure my parents could attest [to] this, knows that I put more pressure on myself than anybody could hope to."

The appointment of Kreis was an important milestone for New York City FC. However, with many front office roles still waiting to be filled, and the team's debut season fast approaching, job descriptions were a fluid concept.

"I was thrown into sponsorship, ticketing, marketing, the logo, fan development, finance, IT, legal," remembers Reyna, who as a player and a technical director had rarely strayed that far into front office operations, "and it was an incredible crash course in business, franchises, sports organisations, and I was learning so much it was amazing."

Even for somebody that had spent most of his life around football clubs in the US, Germany and the UK, the experience of building one from the inside out was a revelation.

"As a player you see your world," explains Reyna. "You're focused on the day-to-day. You take care of yourself, in terms of eating, sleeping, and your family. You work within a group and that's it. That's all you know. You have no idea. And I see it now. As a player I was interested, and I would ask questions and try to understand how a football team was run, but it was night and day in terms of what I know now. It was definitely something I had no idea about until I lived it."

One person who could relate was Patrick Vieira, who played the final two seasons of his career at Manchester City before joining the Club as an executive in 2011, and who later served as Head Coach of New York City FC from January 2016 to June 2018.

"When I decided to follow Brian Marwood for a year, and to spend time in every department in the football club, this is when I first understood that it's not just about the 11 players, or the 26 players in the squad," says Vieira. "There's an organisation working really hard to try to make those 26 players successful. The way that the players conduct themselves, and the results of the team, can have a massive impact on people around the football club. Of course, when you are a player you just focus on winning, losing, playing well, but you don't realise how important it can be for a team to win or lose. Winning, of course, makes jobs easier for people, and losing makes it even more difficult. And as a player, you don't realise the impact that can have on all the people who are working around the football club."

For New York City FC, assembling its own squad of players was the next item on the to-do list.

CHAPTER 15:

A TALE OF TWO SIGNINGS

It is common for football teams to add new players every year. It is rare for any club to set out to recruit an entire playing squad from scratch. However, that is the daunting task that confronted CFG planners less than 18 months out from New York City FC's inaugural MLS season in 2015.

"Well, the first thing you have to think about is the rules," explains New York City FC's Sporting Director, Claudio Reyna. "There's a lot of strategy that goes into the building of a team, in terms of positioning as well. I like to get thoughts and input from a lot of different people, because we have a lot of smart minds, and I think the more you listen, the better."

Squad planning for New York City FC was led by Reyna, Brian Marwood and Head Coach, Jason Kreis, in consultation with Txiki Begiristain. David Lee, the Club's Director of Player Recruitment, was another key figure behind-the-scenes and a resident authority on MLS's complex rules and regulations.

As it geared up for the MLS Expansion Draft in December 2014, where New York City FC [alongside the other incoming expansion team that year, Orlando FC] would source the majority of its players, CFG turned its immediate attention to filling at least two of its three Designated Player slots, which are excluded from the League's salary cap.

With its future rivals watching on, the new franchise didn't disappoint. On 2 June 2014, New York City FC announced that the Spanish World Cup winner, UEFA Champions League winner, and former Valencia, FC Barcelona and Atletico Madrid striker, David Villa, had agreed to become its first ever player.

"That first signing had to be carefully considered," says Chairman, Khaldoon Al Mubarak. "We needed a player that was a proven winner, a superstar, respected around the world, the right age, that we knew would come in and perform immediately, and a star that is hungry. And you know, David Villa was an immediate, perfect fit. He is a World Cup winner. He is a Champions League winner. He's won every trophy that there is in European football. He was the top scorer in every league he's played in. He's an aggressive player, a hungry player. He's in very good physical condition. So, when the opportunity presented itself, it was a no brainer. He would be the perfect fit to start a franchise with. And it was the right call. He's done it again. He's proven to be exactly what we expected he would be."

"I think David is very special in many ways," says Marwood. "I think as a person, and as a footballer, he's brought a level of quality and a best-in-class in terms of this is what playing and training and living your life looks like. He was a teacher for the group. It was a little bit like what we had when Patrick [Vieira] came to Manchester City in 2010."

Vieira joined Manchester City towards the end of his playing career and his towering presence, both on the pitch and in the dressing room, was widely credited with helping the side to convert its promise into silverware.

"With David, this was a guy that was super serious about not just coming to retire and end his career gracefully," says Marwood. "This was a guy that had determination, hunger and desire that was burning brightly every time you met him. This guy was on a mission. He wanted to be the leader of this new club. He wanted to be the figurehead of who we were, what we were doing, how we would do it. He's been a very powerful presence for many different reasons, and a great example to many in this industry that if you live your life the right way, and you do the right things, and you have that desire to compete, it's amazing what you can achieve."

The signing of Villa also sent a clear message to New York City FC's early adopters about what they could expect from the new Club.

"What it said to New York," says CFG board director, Simon Pearce, "was that we'll give you relevant, current competence. We're not going to give you a sentimental journey into football from another era. You know, a 'has been.' We're going to give you somebody who could still play for his country. We're going to give you a New York standard player, and that was really important. It was like, 'This guy wants to be here, he wants to play for you, and he could play for anybody right now.'"

Ferran Soriano agrees and credits Villa for his exceptional work rate.

"There are stories of players that have gone to the US and they haven't worked that much," he says. "Not him. He went there. He continued to work. He scored goals. He was the MVP [in 2016]. He has developed as a true captain. And at the end of the day, this cannot be commercial. A commercial captain is not accepted by the team. The players only accept captains that deliver everything on the pitch, and when things go wrong, have the character, and he is that man."

"You know, he's extremely humble," says Villa's teammate, Tommy McNamara, who was still in his final year of college when the establishment of New York City FC was publicly announced, and who ended up joining the new Club via the MLS Expansion Draft in December 2014. "Even though he's won essentially everything there is to win in soccer, he treats everybody the same. He doesn't look down on people and he doesn't need to do what the person next to him does."

He may have had the character and experience to wear the captain's armband, but when Villa first arrived in the US, he spoke very little English.

"Yeah," recalls Villa, in an interview conducted entirely in English at the Club's former training base at SUNY Purchase, "when I arrived here, I didn't speak nothing. I tried to do classes with my teacher for months before I started pre-season. When we started pre-season, I spoke a little bit, nothing serious. I tried to learn from my team mates, from the people working in the Club, and day-by-day I improved a little bit, and finally I'm here to talk… badly… but I'm happy for my English, and I can be better."

According to CFG's Vicky Kloss, who speaks four languages herself, the only player that she has ever seen learn English as quickly as David Villa was the Argentine defender, Pablo Zabaleta, who joined Manchester City in 2008.

Villa's adjustment to life in New York City appears to have been aided by a 'take it as it comes' attitude that seems at odds with the attention to detail he brings to his match day preparation.

"In my life, I never expect anything before it happens," explains Villa. "I will always try. Go to the city, or go to the situation, and see what happens there. When you expect something, it can be good sometimes, and it can be bad sometimes, because you expect a lot and it's short, or in the opposite, you expect less and you are surprised with more. In my life, I always try to never expect anything. Go there, live life, see what happens in the situation."

After three seasons, 63 goals, 21 assists and an MLS MVP award in 2016, Villa seems satisfied with how things have worked out. In May 2017, he signed a one-year extension with New York City FC that will keep him at the Club until the end of the 2018 season.

"Of course, I am so happy," says Villa, "and it's a pleasure to live here and play for NYCFC. It's a great opportunity for me, it's a great opportunity for my family, and for my kids, to be here."

Things didn't go as smoothly for New York City FC's second designated player and fourth player signed overall, former Chelsea legend and 106-game England veteran, Frank Lampard.

On 24 July 2014, a New York City FC press release entitled 'Welcome to New York: Frank Lampard,' quoted the midfielder as saying: "It is a privilege to be able to help make history here in New York City – I just can't wait to get started and be part of it." As it turned out, it would be almost an entire year before Lampard would make his long-awaited debut for New York City FC, after controversially remaining in England for the first half of the MLS season and playing instead for Manchester City.

"I signed Frank with Ferran," recalls Marwood. "We'd agreed everything in London. I think we'd signed him when he was out of contract in the summer, and then literally it became a situation of, 'Well, where are you going to train until pre-season starts in January?' It was really just about him keeping fit and being ready for the start of the season."

"With Lampard we had the same problem that we had with Villa," explains Soriano, "which is that he was free in the summer, but could not play in New York until March. So, he had to go somewhere. With Villa, we decided to send him to

Melbourne. With Frank, we couldn't do it, because in Melbourne there was only one place for a guest player, so we thought he could do Manchester."

It wasn't an easy sell at first.

"He had it in his mind that he was never going to play for another English club," says Marwood, "because his passion and love for Chelsea was there, and still is, for everybody to see, and he didn't like the thought of playing against Chelsea. But I think, you know, he wasn't in the Premier League, and then he was here and he was training with really good players. It began to pull on him a little bit."

When called into action by then Manchester City Manager, Manuel Pellegrini, Lampard was remarkably effective, scoring four goals in his first four games.

"The problem is that he did so well, that at the end of the period, the coach in Manchester asked us for him to stay," says Soriano.

Lampard's brief stint at Manchester City ended up lasting for more than eight months.

"That turned into something really good for Manchester," says Marwood, "because he ended up playing some big games for us, and he actually scored against Chelsea [in September 2014, without celebrating out of respect for his former club], but it then became a huge problem for New York. And that was two-fold. It was a PR nightmare to deal with, but more importantly, we didn't have him on the pitch, and that was tough."

"We had to take a difficult decision," says Soriano, "because the coach in Manchester was asking us for Frank to stay, and we thought actually, you know, there's plenty of examples of players that go to MLS in the middle of the season. It's not a big deal. But obviously, when you take this decision, you don't know what's going to happen in Manchester or what's going to happen in New York with the team. And we had a backlash in New York."

The backlash largely stemmed from the fact that, although Lampard had originally been presented as a New York City FC signing, CFG was somehow able to keep him in Manchester once it decided that was where he could be of most use to the Group.

Three years later, CFG officials appear torn over the incident and the way that it was handled at the time.

"As a decision, it was always going to be catastrophic [from a communications perspective]," says Kloss, who was called upon to help manage the aforementioned backlash. "There was no way of making this a nice announcement, but the challenging thing was that we were interpreted as being liars, and trying to cover something up, which wasn't true. So, it was a bloody nose to some degree."

They may not have been liars, but in January 2015, CFG did publicly clarify that "The statement on the NYCFC website in July [2014] saying Lampard's two-year contract [with NYCFC] took effect from Aug 1, 2014 was a mistake." Compounding the issue, City admitted that a separate statement that had appeared temporarily on the Manchester City website, reporting that Lampard was "on loan" with the English club, had also been technically incorrect.

Lampard soon issued a statement of his own to clarify that he had signed a "commitment" to join New York City as of 1 January 2015, before agreeing to be part of the Manchester City squad on an interim basis, presumably on a 12-month contract [the shortest allowable under Premier League rules]. CFG added that Lampard's "commitment" to New York City FC [which it referred to as a "Head of Terms commitment"] had been extended to the end of the 2014-15 season, and that any playing contract between him and the MLS club would not begin until 1 July 2015. The Premier League weighed in to confirm that none of their rules had been broken, but that they considered Lampard to be on a one-year deal with Manchester City.

It was utterly confusing, and a bad look for everybody involved, but particularly for CFG.

"In hindsight, obviously, it didn't work that well," says Soriano, of Lampard's extended stay in England, "because in Manchester he helped more in the first half of the season than the second, and then when he went to New York, he got injured. His adaptation was not that easy."

"My real, honest point of view," says Reyna, looking back on New York City FC's inaugural season in 2015, "is that if Frank was there from the beginning of the year, playing with us, I'm pretty confident that we get that much closer to making the playoffs. I couldn't replace him, because he was still part of the roster. With Frank, I really think we could have made the playoffs."

"He should have gone," says Pearce in hindsight. "There was an anomaly in the fact that Pellegrini wanted to keep him, and he did us proud in the Premier League. [But] if we had our time again, I'd have said he should have gone, because he would have made a difference."

When asked to weigh up the Lampard situation three years later, Marwood sighs.

"Right decision for Manchester," he says. "Wrong decision for New York."

The supporters of both clubs would probably agree.

CHAPTER 16:

THE HOME OPENER

Less than two years after the deal was signed to create a new football team in New York City, the final countdown was underway. New York City FC would play its first home game on 15 March 2015. Everything that could be managed was under control. The one thing that couldn't almost led to the cancellation of the game.

"That was one of the harshest winters that the North East had ever had," remembers Tom Glick, CFG's Chief Commercial Officer, who served as President of New York City FC from January 2015 to March 2016, "and there was this big build-up of snow over December [2014] and January [2015], and it just stayed cold, so it wasn't melting."

The big freeze put a hold on the removal of the grass inside Yankee Stadium and the laying of new turf for the upcoming MLS season.

"It snowed a lot," says Glick, "and that continued through February and into March, and the problem we had is that it was all of the North East. So, what we needed was for the snow to melt, and then we needed to get enough sod to replace the turf, in order to be able to play our games, and the problem we had is that all of the sod farms in the North East were also frozen."

With the 2015 MLS season now only weeks away, CFG soon found itself heading further and further south in search of useable grass for its pitch.

"We were looking all the way down into North Carolina, South Carolina, Georgia, for sod that we could use that was warm," says Glick, "and that matched up with the kind of grass that we needed, because if you go too far south you lose the Kentucky Bluegrass and you start getting into Bermuda grass, which is the wrong kind of grass."

City eventually sourced its sod and in late February the cold broke long enough for the Yankees to remove the dead grass that was still in the Stadium.

"Anyway, we got all that done," says Glick, who clearly learned more about the finer points of growing grass during this period than he cared to know. "We got the snow off, we got the sod laid, and then it snowed again the week before the game, and we were concerned that there was going to be snow on the pitch. Ultimately, we went into the first week of the season not knowing if we were actually going to get the game in, including when we flew down to Orlando for our very first game [on 8 March 2015]."

Claudio Reyna couldn't believe it.

"We were sitting in the boardroom here [at the NYCFC office]," he says, "and I remember Tom Glick was saying there is a potential that we may need to cancel the game. It was everyone's worst nightmare. It had all been gearing up to this and we wanted to get the first game in."

Before departing for Orlando, Reyna visited Yankee Stadium to inspect the surface for himself.

"They said, 'You've got to come down and see the pitch,'" he recalls.

As he walked out across centrefield, Reyna was shocked by what he saw.

"I literally went, 'Holy [expletive],'" he says. "The whole field was ripped up. They were still clearing snow. There was a small digger, ripping up the grass and taking it out. I looked at it and said, 'Oh my god, there's no chance we're playing this game.'"

Also at Yankee Stadium that day, CFG's Jon Stemp and Tony Lynn, were more optimistic.

"I grabbed Tony," says Reyna, "and I'm like, 'We're not playing this game. There's no way. Look at this field!' And he was trying to stay positive. He was like, 'We'll get there.' And Jon being ever the optimist kept saying, 'Be positive, they're going to get it done, these guys are amazing. It's the Yankees!'"

"We've got a history of saying, 'Don't worry, it will be okay,'" explains Stemp, who has overseen an array of small and large infrastructure projects on behalf of Manchester City and CFG since 2008. "It's really important that Claudio and the team have no doubts that it will be ready. It's our job to not only get it done, but to reassure them that it's going to be okay."

He may have been reassured, but Reyna wasn't convinced.

"I was like, 'Oh Jon, no way,'" he recalls. "This is not happening.'"

In the end though, Jon was right. The Yankees got it done, and the game went ahead after all. Footage from the match reveals an off-colour playing surface that partially resembles a patchwork quilt.

For many of the people that had been involved in the establishment of New York City FC, the Club's inaugural home opener at Yankee Stadium was an emotional occasion.

"It was a wonderful day," recalls Chairman, Khaldoon Al Mubarak, "but honestly, I remember going to that game not knowing what to expect. You know, almost in no man's land. Was this going to work? What was the environment going to be like? How will the fans react? I didn't have expectations, because I wasn't sure what to expect. I mean, how many times in your life do you actually build a new franchise, and attend the first game of a new franchise that didn't exist?"

Looking out from the Owners' Suite at Yankee Stadium, Soriano was struck by the sea of blue making its way into the ground.

"I think we had 44,000 people, and the big majority of them were wearing the blue shirt," he says.

Vicky Kloss was also stunned by the proud display of blue.

"I could not compute that this football club did not exist, as a playing football club, a week before, a day before," she says, "but that there were forty thousand people, many of whom were clad, head-to-toe in this City gear, and they were screaming their lungs out as if they'd supported this team for thirty years."

New York City FC sold a record 12,704 items of merchandise at its home opener alone – including 3,500 scarves on a bracing sub-40°F night in the Bronx – and would go on to top the League in stadium and online merchandise sales over the course of the

2015 season [with four New York City FC players – Pirlo, Villa, Lampard and Diskerud – appearing among the 10 highest-selling MLS jerseys that year].

Less than an hour before the first home game got underway, Soriano discreetly slipped out of the official pre-match function, rode an elevator downstairs on his own, and took a walk around Yankee Stadium to soak up the atmosphere outside the arena.

"I did all the things I needed to do," he explains, "to greet people and everything. Then I went alone to walk around the Stadium. This was a very emotional day for me, because this was an idea brought to reality. And when I saw the long lines of people dressed in blue, I felt a very strong emotion."

One scene that sticks with him to this day is a conversation he overheard between a father and son as they patiently waited in line to enter the venue.

"The boy was like six years old," remembers Soriano, "and they were both wearing the shirt, the blue shirt. And the son asked the father, 'Why are we wearing this?' And the father told the boy, 'This is the team of your city. This is your team.' And when I heard that I thought, 'We won. That's it. That's the ultimate objective. This is the realisation of our success.'"

For Edelman, the only American on the CFG Board, that first home game was also a patriotic experience.

"We knew we'd have a big crowd," says Edelman, "but we sold the Stadium out. The noise was fantastic. You could feel that it was something really special. But for me, it was when they played the Star-Spangled Banner, which in America is always a special moment when you go to a sporting event. It was like, 'Wow. This is really great.'"

"Yankee Stadium's seen a lot of great moments," says Randy Levine, President of the New York Yankees. "A lot of great moments. And to have a new franchise make its inaugural there, I thought was extraordinarily exciting. There was a real buzz and electricity in the Stadium. It was a great game."

Even the players, schooled from an early age to say that each game is just as important as any other, are prepared to admit that this was a special night.

"The highlight of the year was our opening game at Yankee Stadium," says Tommy McNamara, without hesitation. "You know, we weren't exactly sure how well received we were going to be, and how many people were going to support the Club."

"We were a little bit nervous," concedes captain David Villa, who is anything but a shrinking violet, "because we didn't know that so many people would come to watch our game. It's the first game in our history, the team didn't exist five months ago, and it's always hard to find your supporters. But this day, it was I think 44,000 people. It was amazing, and a very cold day, but it was nice. It was one of the best moments in our history."

When the game kicked off, it wasn't just the number of fans that stood out.

"The atmosphere was something I'll never forget, because it was loud with energy," recalls Reyna, who has played on many of the game's biggest stages himself both at club level and with the US national team, "but it was also a crowd that understood football. They were booing bad calls. They were really into the game in the right way."

According to Reyna, watching soccer in the US hadn't always been this way.

"Ten years earlier," he says, "the loudest cheer was when the goalie kicked it in the air 50 yards."

That night in Yankee Stadium, it was clear that things had changed.

"For me, to see fans that actually understood the game," says Reyna, "that if a nice pass was made they would clap it, and if it was a nice chance, they were 'oohing' and 'ahhing' at the right moments, that was something that gave me a lot of comfort to say, 'Wow, we have real fans in here.'"

In fact, by the time of New York City FC's first home game in March 2015 at least five independent fan groups had sprung into existence, including recognised supporters group, The Third Rail.

New York City FC went on to win its first home game 2-0. David Villa scored in the 19th minute and played a key role in the second [scored by Patrick Mullins] in the 84th minute.

"Yeah, it was important," says Villa of that first home goal, "because I remember that we left for the pitch a little bit nervous from the pressure of everybody knowing that this is our first game. For New England [Revolution] it was their first game against us, but it was not the first game in their history. And the goal, I think, calmed us down."

By the time the final whistle blew, New York City FC couldn't have hoped for a better home debut.

"Somehow, everybody pulled it off," says Reyna. "Everything came together, and it was a special moment. The players getting the win. David was amazing, our first home goal – Mix Diskerud scored our first ever goal [against Orlando City FC on 8 March 2015] – and it was beautiful. We even had, I remember, incredible saves that kept us in the game. We could have been a goal down, but we ended up scoring. It was an amazing day for the Club, absolutely."

"And as we left at the end of the game," recalls Kloss, "which was the perfect result and all the rest of it, there were people in the streets in these huddles, like you see in shots of the World Cup, in little squares and plazas, with flags and face paint, going "Championes," almost! I was like, 'I can't believe it. I can't. There's not a history to this yet, and this is what it has inspired.'"

"I mean, you couldn't write it, huh?" says Al Mubarak, reflecting on that memorable night. "Opening day. Great crowd. Win. And David Villa scores the first goal."

"It's not bad," adds Simon Pearce.

"It's not bad," agrees Al Mubarak. "You couldn't possibly have dreamed it up that way."

CHAPTER 17:

THE EARLY LESSONS

Pride comes before a fall. And after the high of New York City FC's euphoric home debut, the team then went the next 11 games without a win. By season's end, New York City FC had failed to qualify for the play-offs in its inaugural season, finishing eighth in MLS's Eastern Conference and 17th overall with 10 wins, seven draws and 17 losses.

The outcome was disappointing but not entirely unexpected.

"So, we win our first home game," recalls Brian Marwood, "and you go, 'Wow, this is what this could be like.' But I knew that day that this was going to be a tough season, because you could just sense that we probably didn't have the team that could compete at the top, top level. And this Group is about winning. New York City has got to be a winning team, as Manchester City is, and I didn't feel, from a football perspective, that the team then was capable of winning."

Although it wasn't always pretty, the team learned some valuable lessons from its inconsistent first season.

"We learned a lot of things on the sporting side," says David Villa. "We learned that it's hard to build a team in the first year, because all the guys in the team are new. This is not normal. Normally teams in pre-season have five, six, seven new guys, but never a full team. It was a difficult season for us, but it was good for growing in the future."

"It was very difficult," agrees Tommy McNamara. "When we came into pre-season, maybe a couple of guys had played together before, but to try to get everybody on the same page in a fairly short pre-season, it's difficult. And then when you start adding in injuries, new guys coming into the team and out of the team. It's tough. It's a lot tougher than when you're on the outside looking in."

Playing in his first MLS season, Villa also gained a greater understanding of the unique rigours of the competition.

"It's a league that is very physical," he says, "and it's a league that changes the times you play. Normally in Europe, in summer you are playing at night, here [in the US] you are playing at two'o'clock [in the afternoon] sometimes."

The vastness of the United States can be a challenge on its own.

"For example," says Villa, "the last game we played was against Colorado. We flew four hours, plus one hour before in the airport, plus one hour on the bus to the airport, and the day after we're playing 2500m [above sea level] in Colorado in the mountains. The day after this trip. This doesn't happen in Europe."

However, what stood out most for Villa in his first season – and will be music to the ears of those calling the shots at MLS headquarters – was the unrelenting competitiveness of the League.

"It's a difficult league," he says, "because here we don't have a Real Madrid or a Barcelona. Every team can beat you. You need to play one hundred per cent every game. These things don't happen to the best teams in Europe. You need to always be one hundred per cent if you want to beat teams, because the difference between the first team on the table and the last team is so small."

From the perspective of CFG, the extent to which New Yorkers embraced the new franchise was encouraging.

"I think we learned that New York is alive to soccer," says Tom Glick. "The season ticket base grew to 20,000 by the end of the year. The crowds, we averaged 29,000 [3rd in the League in 2015]. People had fun. They liked Yankee Stadium as a venue. While everybody is ready for us to have a soccer-specific stadium, that [playing at Yankee Stadium] worked. So, I think we learned that New York is a soccer city, and this was extremely encouraging. I think intuitively we thought this would be the case, and we were hopeful. But you know, you just don't know until you roll it out."

It wasn't all quiet reflection, with New York City FC also making some high-profile personnel changes after one season, most notably, parting company with Head Coach, Jason Kreis, on 2 November 2015.

"It's always sad when those things come to an end," says Marwood, "because you're dealing with people's lives, and he is a really genuine, honest guy. I think he kind of felt like he was letting us down with some of the results, but history will tell you it's very rare for a franchise to come out of the starting blocks and be successful. It just doesn't normally happen, and I think it was tough for him on many fronts."

Although few people realised it at the time, the announcement of Patrick Vieira as the incoming Head Coach of New York City FC on 9 November 2015 [a role he would hold from January 2016 to June 2018] represented more than just a change in manager. It also signaled a whole new mindset for CFG in its strategic approach to MLS.

"This is an interesting story," explains Soriano, "because we've learned, collectively, over the years, that we might have given too much importance to the specifics of US soccer. We decided [in advance of the 2015 season] that we needed a US coach that really understood the League, because the League was different, and was more physical."

For a number of reasons, the plan didn't work out.

"So, we changed our mind," said Soriano. "Over time we've come to the understanding that soccer is soccer everywhere, and you just need talent and intelligence, and it works. So, three years later, we had a French coach that had no idea about the MLS [when he came to the League], and we had players that were less physical and more talented."

Statistics confirm that New York City FC entered the 2017 season with a 28-player roster that, on average, was marginally shorter [by three inches], lighter [by five pounds] and younger [by two years] than the Club's inaugural 30-player roster in 2015. The 2017 squad was also more international in its composition, featuring players from 16 different countries [up from nine in 2015].

In June 2018, Vieira announced his departure from New York City FC in order to take up the role as Manager of French Ligue 1 club, OGC Nice. CFG officials were visibly saddened to learn that Vieira was leaving the City organisation after eight years there as a player, executive and coach, with at least two senior figures suggesting that he may one day return in another capacity. Domenec Torrent, who has worked alongside Pep Guardiola for more than a decade [at FC Barcelona, Bayern Munich and most recently, Manchester City], was appointed Head Coach of New York City FC on 11 June 2018.

In its first three MLS campaigns, New York City FC has made the play-offs twice [knocked out both times in the conference semi-finals]. Although it is yet to have its own stadium, in April 2018, the Club shifted its football operations to a bespoke new training facility [the Etihad City Football Academy] in Orangeburg, New York.

At the time of writing, New York City FC has more than 16,000 season ticket holders, and is slowly but surely carving out its own place in the hearts and minds of the people of New York City.

"I think in New York you have to have confidence or you get run over," says Reyna, "but at the same time, you have to have humility. I think we've developed that confidence and sort of that bravado that you need to survive in New York, but at the same time, not being a team that walks around boasting, bragging, thinking we're better than anybody else."

"I'm used to walking around the city and seeing Yankee hats and Yankee jerseys and Yankee sweatshirts," says Randy Levine, President of the New York Yankees, "and now I smile because, not only walking around the city do I see Yankee apparel, I see a lot of people wearing New York City Football Club apparel. And once that starts to take hold, it means the franchise is taking hold, and starting to become a foundation of the New York City sports scene."

However, from the perspective of CFG, this is only the beginning of a much longer journey.

"We're building history," says Al Mubarak. "I firmly believe that soccer is going to grow and become the second most popular sport in America. Now, does it happen in 10, 20 or 30 years? To be honest, I don't know. But my common sense tells me, it is the most popular sport in the world. It is the most popular sport in America in the under-16 age group. It is the most popular unisex sport. So, from my perspective, it's a no-brainer to invest in soccer in America, and to invest in a franchise in MLS."

With a foothold firmly established in a major metropolis such as New York City, CFG is well-positioned to benefit from the expected growth of professional soccer in the US in the future.

"This is not a market, it's a city," stresses Soriano, whose arrival in Manchester in 2012 was the catalyst for a dramatic acceleration in City's global expansion. "And this is not a brand, it's a football club. A million people in New York love soccer. You give them a platform, and they develop something that belongs to the city, is rooted in the city, and is going to last forever."

CHAPTER 18

SISTER CITIES

While CFG was still in the process of securing the expansion licence for New York City in 2013, the emerging football group was already looking for new opportunities to bring additional clubs into its ecosystem.

To the surprise of many, the first place that CFG went after New York City was Melbourne, Australia, through the acquisition of Melbourne Heart FC and its rebranding as Melbourne City FC in 2014.

"Australia was opportunistic," says CFG Chairman, Khaldoon Al Mubarak. "I mean, I don't think we sat down and said, 'You know what? We've looked around the world, and Australia is the first place we're going to invest in.' No, it wasn't that. We had decided that the global idea made sense, and that the City Football Group concept needed to be tested, and Australia came up as an opportunity that was a relatively safe, manageable and risk-controlled testing ground for that new vision. It came up, we took the opportunity, and then it grew from there."

Ferran Soriano says CFG first considered investing in China, but eventually settled on Australia as its initial launching pad into Asia.

"At the time, the way we were thinking about expanding was by looking at two elements," he explains. "The first element was the size of the market and its potential for future growth, so we were looking at places where we thought that football and sports in general were going to grow, like China or India, and places where football was not the number one sport, but we believed it could grow to become the number one or number two sport, like the US and Australia."

On the basis of this first element, CFG decided that China represented the greatest potential opportunity, and began exploring the concept of investing in a club in a major Chinese city.

"However, the other factor that we had to consider was stability," says Soriano, "so places where the league was solid, and that was one of the things that eventually led us to Australia. Australia was a stable environment. At that time, the Chinese league was not as well-organised and professionalised as it is now. So, we went for Australia, which at that time was more similar to New York. There was an opportunity in Sydney, but ultimately we found an opportunity in Melbourne that we liked very much."

Melbourne Heart was established in 2009 as the second A-League team to set up shop in Australia's second largest city. It entered the competition a year later in 2010, and made the finals just once in its first three seasons, before its founders began quietly making plans to sell the Club.

The opportunity to acquire Melbourne Heart was brought to CFG in late 2013 by Bart Campbell, the Chairman of National Rugby League side, the Melbourne Storm, which shared a stadium with the four-year-old football club, who had become aware that its owners were looking to exit.

"I'd heard that City Football Group were looking at an A-League club in Sydney," says Campbell, "and I had already seen what they had done in New York. So, I met up with Simon [Pearce], and I said, 'I know you're focusing your efforts on a team in Sydney, but just for the record, there is an opportunity with a club in Melbourne, and we would be interested in partnering with you to provide some in-market support here,' and that didn't sound entirely crazy to him."

Pearce confirmed CFG's interest in the opportunity, but thought having Campbell front the deal gave the two parties a much better chance of getting the Club for a reasonable price. ADUG and its officials knew from experience that the mere mention of 'Manchester City' or 'Abu Dhabi' tended to give wide-eyed sellers unreasonable expectations for the value of their assets.

"I told Bart that the problem for me is that every time we get close to something, somebody is going to put an 'Abu Dhabi premium' on it, and we are not going to overpay," explains Pearce. "I said, 'We are not anybody's fools. So, if you are prepared to front that for me, then let's talk about you and your partners coming in as minority shareholders.'"

Campbell agreed, and negotiations proceeded on the basis that the owners of the Melbourne Storm would own 80% of Melbourne Heart, and the remaining 20% would be held by an unnamed Premier League club. It was only when the deal was almost done that Campbell revealed to the sellers that the 80/20 split would in fact be the other way around. CFG would own the lion's share of the Club, and the Melbourne Storm ownership would be the minority shareholder.

Melbourne Heart was duly sold to CFG and its minor partners for AU$11.25m on 23 January 2014. Later that day, Melbourne Heart CEO, Scott Munn, received an ominous phone call from CFG director, Simon Pearce, asking him to gather his senior leadership team and bring them to the Crown Hotel [a high-end hotel and casino complex in Melbourne] for an urgent meeting with the new ownership.

"Simon said to me 'Look, can you get your Head of Commercial, Head of Football, Head of Finance and yourself, and come and meet us at the Crown in the city?' So, I went and got them all, and I remember Brad Rowse [the Club's Head of Commercial] in particular was like, 'This is it. They are going to sack us all today,'" recalls Munn.

Rowse doesn't deny he was bracing for bad news.

"My thoughts were that, normally when you get a big corporate takeover, they would get rid of the executive team and put their own people in," says Rowse. "So, we were having a bit of a talk in jest, but also with a bit of concern as well. We were thinking, 'Well, what are you going to do next?'"

"Clearly, we're nervous," admits Munn, laughing about the incident four years later, "and Brad's like, 'Let's stick together, and if they try to ask us to come up individually, we'll all go as one!'"

"We'd also been told two'o'clock or something," adds Rowse, "and then it drifted out to almost four in the afternoon, and we were still sitting there in this hotel lobby, and the longer it went on, the more bleak it looked for us."

"Eventually they called us up," says Munn, "and it was Ferran [Soriano], Simon [Pearce] and Brian [Marwood]. Simon and Ferran spoke, and then Simon said, 'I am going to ask you one question, and I want each of you to answer it.'"

"He said, 'I want you to tell me what keeps you awake at night,' and he started with the first person. It was Paul Jeffrey [Head of Finance], and Paul said 'Cash flow. We have no cash flow, we have to scrimp and save to find the money to pay the wages on the 15th of every month.'"

"Simon said, 'No problem. We have your bank details and tomorrow morning there will be enough cash in the bank for the next 12 months.'"

"Paul says, 'Okay, fantastic. I'll sleep well tonight.'"

"Then he went to Brad and asked the same question, and Brad said 'We've had [Australia's oldest bank] Westpac as our major sponsor for five years and they have just told us they are not going to renew front-of-shirt next year. Simon said, 'No problem. We think Etihad wants to take front-of-shirt next year,' and Brad was like, 'Okay, great.'"

"He then went to John Didulica [General Manager, Football], and John said, 'We finished second-to-last [in 2012-13], and we're at the bottom of the table now.' Simon said, 'Well, we've just won the Premier League, and Brian is going to fix your football department.' John said, 'That's fine with me.'"

"Then they asked me," recalls Munn, "and I said, 'Nothing, because you've just fixed everything that kept me awake at night.'"

Munn, who remains CEO of Melbourne City FC today, says the light-hearted exchange was an important moment.

"It was a bit of an icebreaker," he says, "because at that point we started thinking, 'Okay, these guys seem like good people.' I remember both Brian and Simon spoke about wanting the Club to be successful. They said things like, 'We want to invest. We want to give you an opportunity to succeed. We are not here to come in and judge people by what's happened in the past. We are not here to come in and sack people. We are just going to understand the business. We are going to understand the people. Then we'll make it right, and some things we'll get wrong, and then we'll change it and start again.'"

The message was reassuring. However, Munn admits that he and his colleagues still harboured some doubts as they left that hotel suite high above Melbourne's Yarra River.

"I remember leaving," says Munn, "and a few of us were joking and saying, 'Sure, we're just going to suck all your brains and get three months out of you, and then we're going to sack you,' and all that sort of stuff, but the reality is that those comments of 'We just want to understand the business, and we want to understand the people, and the good people will be able to blossom, and those that can't embrace it will move on,' that is pretty much the reality of what's happened."

For some of CFG's first boots on the ground, the modest atmosphere they found in Melbourne was eerily familiar.

"It felt like a much smaller-scale Manchester City around the time ADUG had taken it over," says Marwood, who audited Melbourne Heart's football department immediately after the takeover. "It was a club that was obviously operating on a very small budget. Basically, the CEO, Scott [Munn], and John Didulica, the Football Director, were doing ten roles each. It was great because it had a real community spirit and no kind of hierarchy with stuff. No matter who you were, everybody just kind of mucked in and got stuff done. One minute John was doing the contracts for the players, and the next minute he's serving them lunches or getting the kit washed. It was a big removal from where we'd got to in Manchester by then."

"It was obviously not an ideal office environment," recalls CFG's Tom Glick, who visited the Club shortly after the acquisition to evaluate its commercial capabilities. "It was far from the stadium, which was not traditional, and it was a small staff that was doing a lot and wearing a lot of hats. I related to it though, especially with some of the things I had done and places I had been earlier in my career, coming up through Minor League Baseball. You could sense that they were a group of people that was surviving, but at the same time there was this real commercial competency. One of the things I remember is their sponsorship team was the best in the League. They were selling more than anybody else, yet had this team that was finishing eighth, ninth, tenth in the table."

Don Dransfield, who was redeployed from New York to Melbourne immediately after the acquisition to lead the development of a business plan for CFG's newest club, had a similar experience when he attended his first A-League game in the small country town of Albury within days of his arrival.

"I'd received all the financials from this guy called 'P.J.' [Paul Jeffrey] and they were brilliant," recalls Dransfield. "They were really professionally done. I hadn't met him yet though, so when I got to the game, Scott said he would introduce me to him. We then ran along and went to the merchandise store, and 'P.J.' was there selling shirts. This guy was the financial controller for the Club. He'd done all of the due diligence stuff for the sale to a really professional standard, but he was also the guy selling shirts and taking cash on match day. I couldn't believe that."

That combination of competency and goodwill was one of the main reasons why CFG ultimately decided to integrate the Melbourne Heart staff into the Group rather than to outsource many its non-football operations to the Melbourne Storm [the National Rugby League club owned by CFG's minority partner in the transaction], as had been originally considered. According to Soriano, the learnings from that integration process continue to deliver benefits to the Group today.

"It was important," says Soriano, "because the value of our investment in Australia was obviously the team itself, but also the fact that it enabled us to create the Group mechanism that we needed. As a result, I think today we have a system where we can add a new club, I am not going to say effortlessly, but with a reasonable amount of effort, and it is not a drama. This is because we now have the systems on the football side, on the commercial side, and on the IT side, that allow us to do this."

Dransfield agrees that the significance of the Melbourne acquisition has always been greater than the sum of its price.

"Melbourne didn't complete the story, but it at least allowed us to start to tell the story," he says, of Melbourne's strategic importance to CFG at the time. "Before then, we just had these two anchor assets. This big Premier League club [Manchester City FC], and then this big and obviously very expensive asset in a prime city in the US [New York City FC]. What Melbourne allowed us to do in a relatively inexpensive way was to complete that part of the arc, but in a salary-capped environment where you didn't have some of the issues around match fixing, corruption and other allegations that you had in a lot of the markets that we were looking at. It was a smart, low cost way of doing that."

Melbourne Heart was renamed Melbourne City FC in June 2014 and CFG bought out its minority shareholder the following year to own 100% of the Club.

The next stop for the emerging CFG was ten hours flying time away in Yokohama, Japan.

In July 2014, CFG announced an unusual partnership with Nissan that saw the

Japanese automaker become a global sponsor of CFG, two months after CFG had bought a 20 per cent stake in the Nissan-owned J-League club, Yokohama F. Marinos.

"The Yokohama arrangement is probably a different model because that one was born off the back of our commercial deal with Nissan," says Marwood. "Nissan owned Yokohama Marinos, and they were very open with us saying, 'Listen, we make cars, but we've got this football club that is part of our DNA, because it's right in the heart of Yokohama, and we'd like you to help us with its football operations.'"

"The club was struggling," says Omar Berrada, now Manchester City's Chief Operating Officer. "It was struggling financially and it was struggling on the pitch. That's when the idea came up of, 'Okay, if we came in and helped you make the club more successful, would you come in as a global sponsor?'"

That double coincidence of wants remains at the heart of the CFG-Nissan partnership today.

"So, as part of the relationship," explains Berrada, "we bought a stake [in Yokohama F. Marinos], and committed to helping them on two fronts. First, on the commercial side, by leveraging our global sales network to help bring them sponsors, and second, helping them on the football front."

Three years after Yokohama, the next two clubs to join CFG were Uruguay's Club Atlético Torque [100 per cent owned by CFG under an agreement signed in April 2017] and Spain's Girona FC [44.3 per cent owned by CFG since August 2017].

The investment in Girona FC is already paying dividends, with CFG officials estimating that the Club has quadrupled in value since securing promotion from the Spanish Second Division and staying up after its first season in La Liga in 2017-18. The connection to Girona FC has been beneficial in other ways, with Manchester City's Pablo Maffeo sold to Stuttgart FC in May 2018 for £8.8m with a 25 per cent sell-on clause, after playing the last two seasons on loan at the Spanish club.

The rationale behind CFG's acquisition of Club Atlético Torque is at least partly geographical.

"Torque gives us a foothold into South America," says Al Mubarak. "It's in Uruguay, which has historically been one of the most successful places in terms of producing young talent. It's a good legal jurisdiction and a good economic place to invest, and CFG is uniquely equipped to help the Club succeed and grow."

"Uruguay is a very small country," says Soriano. "Only 3.5 million people. But, they are two-time winners of the World Cup. The amount of good players to have come from there is spectacular. In the case of Torque, this was a very small team. We bought the team, it got promoted to the first division, and we hope that we can develop some very good talent there."

Early signs are positive, with 19-year-old Argentine midfielder Valentin Castellanos moving to New York City FC on loan [with an option to purchase] from Club Atlético Torque in July 2018. Castellanos is not the first, and is unlikely to be the last, promising young player to move from one CFG club to another in order to take the next step in their career.

In early 2014, in a deal negotiated just days before CFG's acquisition of Melbourne City and completed after it, the Club signed a talented Australian midfielder by the name of Aaron Mooy, on a free transfer from another A-League club. In 2016, after two strong seasons at Melbourne City, Mooy was sold to sister club, Manchester City, who immediately loaned him out to Huddersfield Town. There, Mooy was instrumental in the Terriers gaining promotion from the EFL Championship to the Premier League, taking out the Club's Player of the Season award in 2016-17. In June 2017, Huddersfield Town signed Mooy permanently from Manchester City for a fee of £8m [potentially rising to £10m].

The Mooy fee [AU$14-18m] was worth more than the amount that CFG paid for Melbourne City FC [AU$11.25m] in 2014.

CHAPTER 19

CFG TODAY

CFG today is more than just a network of clubs in the UK, US, Australia, Japan, Spain and Uruguay. According to CFG officials, owning and operating football clubs is now just one of the Group's three core activities.

"Ok, so today we have investments in six football clubs, in six countries, on five continents, and all of them are in the top division of their countries," explains CFG CEO, Ferran Soriano. "That is our number one business."

"We have a second area of focus that is the development of players," adds Soriano. "We work with them to develop them to the maximum of their potential, and they can then end up playing in one of our teams at different levels."

In addition to the six clubs that CFG wholly or partially owns, the Group has also established strategic partnerships with clubs such as NAC Breda in the Netherlands, where multiple players from the Manchester City Academy are currently on loan.

"We can now offer a player almost any level of competitiveness to support their development," says Soriano. "Some of these players are going to end up playing for us, and some are going to end up playing for other teams."

The economic rationale behind CFG's involvement in the management of clubs and development of players is obvious. By doing these things at scale, CFG can extract maximum value out of investments in things like scouting and recruitment networks, performance analysis systems, marketing and commercial capabilities, and professional services such as finance, legal and IT. However, CFG's third area of focus is different to the first two, and it is the one that people seem to know the least about.

"So, our third set of businesses are soccer-related businesses that are not clubs or players," explains Soriano. "For example, we have an investment in a company in California called Goals, that manages recreational soccer pitches. We have Schools of Football around the world. We have an interest in e-sports. We are in the process of creating a fund to invest in sports and technology ventures around the world."

"This is who we are today," says Soriano.

CFG officials insist that the Group's underlying premise is less about slapping the word 'City' on clubs, products and services, and more about injecting its assets, capabilities and expertise into a growing range of enterprises that all link back in some way to football, sports and entertainment.

"Everything ultimately comes back to how we can take what we have and do more with it," says board director, Marty Edelman. "So, yes, the investment fund will be a private equity fund, but it will be a private equity fund that is focused on investing in different sports technology platforms that could impact things like the data we can collect, and the content that we can develop at our clubs."

"By necessity, Manchester City became very good at the business of football," explains board director, Simon Pearce, "so when CFG was created, we naturally focused in the beginning on the management of football organisations. What's happened since is that we've broadened our understanding of the football competencies that we have, from player development and coaching development, to things like infrastructure, commercial relationships and the use of technology. We have now ended up in the situation where our investment in clubs is being integrated and cross-pollinated with all of these other areas of expertise."

Although CFG as a whole is yet to deliver a profit, Group officials say privately that it is close to breaking even and they expect it to be profitable within two to three years, with Manchester City already profitable and a number of CFG's international businesses steadily improving in their performance.

"It's a good question," says Don Dransfield, when asked about the Group's financial performance to date. "The majority of CFG's revenue and bottom line contributions come from Manchester City. Actually, it makes money and it has done for a number of years. Melbourne is relatively small from a purely financial perspective. The main financial issue right now is New York, and you can take a short-term view on that, and see that as a major problem. The other way of looking at it is to imagine a world

50 years from now where you have the same level of player in the US as you have playing in the UK today. What would the attendance at New York City FC be then? What would the broadcast revenue in the North American market be? And therefore, what would the implied value of New York City FC be? I still believe it will prove to be a great long-term investment."

Dransfield is not alone. In December 2015, a consortium of Chinese investors led by CMC Holdings bought a minority stake of just over 13 per cent of CFG for US$400m. The deal valued the Group at US$3bn.

"There's no better proof point than our sale to CMC," says Al Mubarak. "I mean, right there, we locked in a valuation at US$3bn. We didn't need to sell, but we sold that stake for two reasons. One, it was important to set a market valuation that endorsed our vision. We need to start having the market understand what we are doing, and there is no better way to do that, I think, than through a real transaction. So, honestly, we did that more to set a benchmark. To set a line in terms of where we were at that point, knowing that we're only going to grow that valuation."

"And two," continues Al Mubarak, "it was a strategic decision for us. The next move is China. China is an immense market. It is also a growing market in football, and we have to have the edge there. In the same way that we created the vision of City Football Group, and it is now getting endorsed as we go, I want us to be the first to get a real breakthrough in China. And in my view, there's no better way to do that than to have a good partner, a strong partner, and a partner that's incentivised to grow with us, because you're not going to invest the sort of money they've invested if you didn't buy into our vision."

Almost seven years after CFG first considered investing in the Far East, the Chairman suggests that CFG's long-awaited move into China will happen sooner rather than later.

"I don't know where we're going to end up in China," says Al Mubarak, "or what shape it's going to take, but I do know that in five years' time, when you and I are having another interview, we're going to be there somewhere. I don't have the answer today, but we are doing everything we can right now to figure it out. We'll see where we are in five years, but we're going to do it. That's the next edge."

MANCHESTER CITY

CHAPTER 20

THIS CHARMING MAN

Manuel Pellegrini was appointed Manager of Manchester City on 14 June 2013. To many, he was a surprising choice to replace the popular Roberto Mancini.

"It was a strange one," says Gary James, a football historian and Manchester City season ticket holder for the last 30 years. "Most of us loved Mancini. I still do. I know we have heard all sorts of rumours, but Mancini was the man who brought us trophies. Obviously, I know it is not as simple as that, but he was perceived as the guy who brought us success. I think most of us realised that he was unlikely to bring us all of the success that we would want, year after year. But, Pellegrini was not the appointment that we expected. Even then there was talk of Pep Guardiola, which obviously was not going to happen at that point, but there was talk of it. And so, Pellegrini was not Mancini, and he was not Pep, but bizarrely he brought this air of authority, this elder statesman feeling."

Manchester City officials have never been coy about the fact that Pellegrini was not necessarily their first choice, with the Club reportedly sounding out former FC Barcelona [and eventual Manchester City] Manager, Pep Guardiola, during his

12-month sabbatical in New York City, to gauge his interest in coming to England, while Mancini was still in the first year of a new five-year contract.

"There was an outreach," admits Chairman, Khaldoon Al Mubarak. "I mean, you have to understand, Ferran and Txiki are obviously very close to Pep. Pep was living in New York at this point, and had made himself clearly available on the market. So, Ferran and Txiki reached out to him, but Pep decided that Bayern Munich was the right option for him at that time."

Al Mubarak says Pellegrini knew.

"It was always a transparent relationship with Manuel," he says. "Let me put it this way. Manuel always knew where we stood on things. There was no ambiguity there. And he was always a gentleman and a supreme professional, from day one. He knew, I think, when we hired him, that had Pep been available, he would have been our priority at that point, and that ultimately if he ever became available, he would always be an option that we would consider. I think he knew that, and he was a professional about it. He respected that decision. But he also knew that we were going to give him an opportunity. We were giving him a three-year contract that we were going to respect, and if things worked out, things would go on from there. So, I think the relationship was built on that understanding from the beginning."

Pellegrini was no mere consolation prize. From the moment he sauntered into Manchester City's Carrington training ground on his first day on the job, black leather briefcase in hand, the understated Chilean commanded the respect of everybody at the Club with his calmness and professionalism. To this day, on the record or off, nobody at Manchester City has a bad word to say about him.

"We needed someone that was going to come in, cool things down and reset the culture," says Al Mubarak. "We knew we had a very talented squad. We had the best squad in the League. We needed some improvements, which we made, but we knew we had a winning team. But, the environment was fractured. So, getting someone with experience that could come in and settle things down, that would play the sort of football that we wanted to go towards, that's where Pellegrini came in. He was going to come in, put the team back together, and bring the spirit back to the dressing room."

"At a Club level, it changed everything," says Manchester City CEO, Ferran

Soriano, "because he was a normal person that would not fight with anybody, had reasonable behaviours and attitudes, and would not create any conflict."

"He brought calmness. He brought serenity. He brought an ability for people to be themselves again," says Marwood, who shifted into a new role at the end of 2012 heading up City Football Services [now Global Football], that would see him working across all CFG clubs. "We needed somebody that could take the club to another level, calm the dressing room and get a response from the players. He was just a lovely man, and very knowledgeable about the game."

Pellegrini may have been a soothing presence in the dressing room, but on the pitch his Manchester City side came to embody a breathtakingly aggressive style of football. In his first season [2013-14], Manchester City won the Premier League and the League Cup [beating Sunderland 3-1 in the final on 2 March 2014]. The Club scored a record 156 goals in all competitions, including 102 goals in the Premier League, which was the second highest tally in the history of the competition. Manchester City also made the Round of 16 in the UEFA Champions League.

"Pellegrini was full on attacking football," says Vincent Kompany. "We didn't have as much possession as today, but we were definitely more offensive. And that's not to discredit anything we're doing today, because what we're doing today is the best, but at this point, we usually attack with five and defend with five. Under Pellegrini, we attacked with seven, defended with three."

Even some staunch Mancini loyalists were thoroughly charmed by the end of the season.

"That first season, to get the success he did, it was like, 'Wow,'" says James. "And not just that, but I think that team performed better than it should have done in the circumstances. Despite the managerial change, it seemed to gel quite quickly and achieve more than the sum of its parts. I know I sound hesitant because, personally I still wanted Mancini, to be fair, but Pellegrini delivered more than I expected Mancini to deliver, so on that basis it was a great change."

Speaking to CityTV in May 2014, Al Mubarak emphasised the dual importance of the attractiveness and the effectiveness of the football played under Pellegrini in his first year at the Club.

"I think it's a testament to Manuel's philosophy in terms of how we want to play football," he said. "How we want to play a game that entertains, but at the same time is effective in terms of achieving results. We played at many times this year beautiful football, entertaining football, attacking football, and we won two competitions, and competed at the highest level in the other competitions."

According to Soriano and Txiki Begiristain, Manchester City's Football Director since November 2012, this had been one of the key reasons for bringing Pellegrini to the Club in the first place.

"From a tactical and technical point of view, he brought a very good and clear style of playing," says Soriano. "Manuel brought the philosophy at a basic level. The ball possession, the high defensive line. His main focus was the defensive line and we did very well that year. We won the League and the League Cup, we scored lots of goals and we played very good football."

"He had played very good football in Villareal, in Real Madrid and in Málaga," adds Begiristain. "Very good football using all the width of the pitch. So, we brought him because he had the same football philosophy that we wanted to implant here, and it worked for the first season. The style of the system was slightly different to what we were used to working with, but the principles were the same."

The strategy didn't come without its risks, and in hindsight there were some early signs that it might not be sustainable.

"It was either we annihilated a team or we'd get done," admits Kompany, "and then we were getting picked off against European teams that were opening up the pitch in possession, and our pressing wasn't as good, and we struggled to recover the ball high up the pitch. But in terms of attacking freedom, in that first season, everybody was hyped up and everything was coming off, and that's when we won the title."

However, it wasn't just European football teams that Manchester City had to worry about.

Five days after winning the 2013-14 Premier League, it was announced that the Club had reached a complex settlement with UEFA over alleged breaches of the European regulator's Financial Fair Play [FFA] regulations. According to UEFA, Manchester City had lost more than the allowable amount over the course of the 2011-12 and 2012-13 seasons, and was therefore subject to a range of financial and

Manchester City deliver a rooftop football pitch at P.S. 72
[Lexington Academy] in East Harlem, July 2010

New York City Football Club is unveiled as the 20th MLS team at P.S. 72 with
Claudio Reyna announced as the Club's first employee, May 2013

Claudio Reyna playing for
Manchester City in 2006

David Villa, with CEO Ferran Soriano, is unveiled
as the first New York City FC player, June 2014

Yankee Stadium awash with blue for New York City
FC's inaugural home opener in March 2015

Patrick Vieira as Head Coach of New York City FC with Chairman Khaldoon Al Mubarak, Vice Chairman Marty Edelman and Sporting Director Claudio Reyna

City Football Group and the Melbourne Storm announce the acquisition of Melbourne Heart [now Melbourne City FC] in January 2014

A supporter of Yokohama F. Marinos, minority-owned by
City Football Group since May 2014

Pablo Maffeo in action for Girona FC, following City
Football Group's investment in the Club in 2017

City Football Group acquires Club
Atlético Torque in April 2017

Aaron Mooy in action
for Melbourne City

FINANCIAL TIMES

WEDNESDAY 2 DECEMBER 2015   WORLD BUSINESS NEWSPAPER   UK £2.70 Channel Islands £3.00; Republic of Ireland €3.00

Drug deals
How Valeant's rapid rise came
unstuck — BIG READ, PAGE 10

Martin Wolf
Understanding the new global
oil economy — COMMENT, PAGE 13

Virtual reality
It really is going to be a very big
deal — JONATHAN MARGOLIS, PAGE 14

Chinese make big play with Man City stake

Chinese investors have made a $400m investment in English Premier League leaders Manchester City just weeks after President Xi Jinping visited the club's academy.

The 13 per cent stake in the team's parent City Football Group taken by a consortium of private equity groups values CFG at $3bn and is the first entry into English football by Chinese investors. The valuation puts City on a par with the market capitalisation of local rivals Manchester United.

Football has become a target for Chinese conglomerates and their wealthy founders, which some analysts see as an effort to curry favour with Beijing.
UK football scores a first page 20
Lombard page 22

$3bn
Valuation of CFG, which owns Manchester City

$400m
Cost of a 13% stake. In 2008 the entire club cost $360m

Briefing

▶ **Pressure on Zurich grows as Senn quits**
Zurich Insurance has been pushed further on to the defensive after chief executive Martin Senn resigned yesterday, forcing the Swiss insurer into a hurried hunt for an external replacement.— PAGE 17, LEX, PAGE 16; ANALYSIS, PAGE 20

▶ **Cabinet clears way for Syria strikes vote**
The cabinet has approved a motion to put before parliament today calling for air strikes in Syria, as Jeremy Corbyn told Labour MPs "there's no hiding place" for those who support the vote.— PAGE 2

▶ **Security increased in Tehran on Isis fears**
Police have flooded Iran's capital amid concerns that the country could become a target for Isis, the Sunni jihadi group it has taken an active role in fighting.— PAGE 9, DENNIS ROSS, PAGE 11

▶ **Bargaining starts over climate accord**
Negotiators in UN talks in Paris confronted a host of divisive issues yesterday as they began work on trying to convert a draft text into an agreement for ministers to finalise next week.— COP21 TALKS, PAGE 7

▶ **Brazilian economy takes further hit**
Brazil's gross domestic product fell a record 4.5 per cent year-on-year in the third quarter amid lower commodity prices, fiscal contraction and the fading of a consumer credit boom.— PAGE 8

▶ **BlueCrest to push out external investors**
The $8bn BlueCrest hedge fund is pushing out its external investors, arguing the industry's fee model is no longer profitable enough, with the fund to become a private investment partnership.— PAGE 17

Relief for City as BoE signals an end to the era of bank bashing

A consortium led by CMC Holdings acquires just over 13% of City Football
Group in December 2015, in a deal valuing the Group at US$3bn

Manuel Pellegrini is appointed Manager of
Manchester City in June 2013

Long serving Club Secretary and now Life President Bernard Halford with Pablo Zabaleta
after the League Cup final in March 2014 which Manchester City won 3-1

Manchester City win their second Premier
League title in three seasons in May 2014

Aerial image of the City Football Academy and wider campus
in East Manchester which opened in December 2014

Chancellor of the Exchequer George Osborne with senior officials from Manchester City, City Football Group
and Manchester City Council, at the opening of the City Football Academy in December 2014

Manchester City and England Captain,
Steph Houghton

Senior Manchester City and CFG officials, including Chairman Khaldoon Al Mubarak, Simon
Pearce, Ferran Soriano, Brian Marwood and Txiki Begiristain, at the Etihad Stadium

Txiki Begiristain, Manchester City Director of Football, former Director of Football at FC Barcelona, and former player with Real Sociedad, FC Barcelona, Deportivo La Coruña and the Spanish national team

New Manager Pep Guardiola is introduced to Manchester City fans at
a special supporter event at the City Football Academy in July 2016

His Highness Sheikh Mansour with Chairman Khaldoon Al
Mubarak and Pep Guardiola in Abu Dhabi in March 2018

His Highness Sheikh Mansour with Chairman Khaldoon Al Mubarak greets Sergio
Agüero during warm weather training in Abu Dhabi in February 2017

Manager Pep Guardiola directs his team from the
sidelines at the Etihad Stadium

Manchester City win the 2017-18 Premier League and set new records for points won and goals scored in a single season in May 2018

Gabriel Jesus scores a dramatic last-minute goal against Southampton in the final game of the 2017-18 season to secure Manchester City a record-breaking 100 points

Manchester City's 'Centurions' during their Trophy
Parade in central Manchester, May 2018

Three stars of Manchester City's evolving squad and 'Centurions,'
Raheem Sterling, Leroy Sané and Kevin De Bruyne

sporting penalties designed to make it "break-even compliant" in a short period of time.

Under the terms of the settlement, Manchester City accepted a potential fine of €60m [€20m of which was paid immediately, €40m of which was withheld but would be returned subject to future compliance], a €60m cap on transfer spending for the 2014 summer transfer window [not including money earned via player sales], a freeze on increases to the Club's wage bill, a reduced squad size of only 21 players [instead of the allowable 25] for the 2014-15 UEFA Champions League, and maximum allowable losses in FFP terms of €20m in 2013-14 and €10m in 2014-15.

The Club issued a terse statement maintaining that it believed it had complied with the FFP regulations, and stating that it could challenge the findings if it wished, but that "our decision to do so must be balanced against the practical realities for our fans, for our partners and in the interests of the commercial operations of the club." It was the football equivalent of settling a case without admitting liability; of accepting the penalty but rejecting the finding. In reality, that distinction meant little to the Club's many critics, who saw the voluntary settlement as long-awaited evidence that Manchester City had been breaking the rules.

In May 2014, a defiant Khaldoon Al Mubarak shared his thoughts on the subject with CityTV.

"They have their view, we have ours," he said. "I disagree with their view, but we are pragmatic. And I think one thing our fans needs to know. We will do, as always, what is best for this Club, for the fans, and if it means sometimes to take a pinch, we'll take a pinch. And we'll move on. And we'll be pragmatic. And know that we have the right model, and we believe in this model, and it is the right model. And at the same time, it will not compromise us, and it will not compromise the strategy that we have started, and that we will continue to implement."

Four years later, FFP remains a sore point at Manchester City. Reflecting on these events today, the settlement with UEFA appears to stick in the craw of the ordinarily unruffled Chairman. This is one wound that appears to have hardened, not healed, with time.

"I still have a very raw feeling about this," he says. "I think we were unfairly treated. We were investing long-term. We were investing in the community. We were investing in the Club. We were doing things the right way. And, I think that made many people uncomfortable, and UEFA took a very harsh stand against us."

Al Mubarak argues that the Club has answered many of its critics over the last ten years.

"Ultimately, as time has shown, we've built a sustainable model at Manchester City. We've built an investment case that makes sense, and we've built something that is good for Manchester, good for the Club, and good for football. I don't think we've damaged or hurt football in any way, shape or form, and I think time has shown that. So, I have nothing good to say about this."

Manchester City reported a net loss of £23m for 2013-14, including a £16m fine to UEFA. The Club delivered an annual profit [£10.7m] for the first time in the ADUG era in 2014-15, and has done so every year since. In April 2017, UEFA refunded Manchester City the additional €40m [£33.4m] withheld in 2014 after the Club met the requirements that were imposed on it at the time.

In December 2015, Michel Platini, then President of UEFA and a leading proponent of FFP, was banned from football-related activities for eight years [reduced to four] over ethics violations unrelated to FFP.[20]

Manuel Pellegrini would never eclipse the success of his first year at Manchester City. In his second season in 2014-15, the Club finished second in the Premier League and was knocked out in the Round of 16 of the UEFA Champions League. In the 2015-16 season, Manchester City won the League Cup for the second time in three years and made the semi-finals of the UEFA Champions League for the first time, but finished a disappointing fourth in the Premier League.

In February 2016, Manchester City confirmed that Pellegrini's tenure would end at the conclusion of the 2015-16 season, with the Club not exercising an option to retain him for an additional year. It was also announced that Manchester City had signed a three-year contract with Pep Guardiola to become the Club's new Manager in advance of the 2016-17 season. Pellegrini had personally made the call to go public with the news four months out from the end of the season, later telling The Guardian's Jamie Jackson that he wasn't sure it had been the right decision, with the disrupted side losing three games on the trot after his impending departure was announced.[21]

Pellegrini won three trophies in three years at Manchester City. In three Premier League seasons, his side scored 256 goals. However, Manchester City officials say that the engineer's lasting legacy at the Club was also significant in terms of the culture and structure that he left behind, and not just the silverware and statistics.

"If you look at the journey to get to where we are right now," says Al Mubarak, "Pellegrini was that bridge. Pellegrini embraced the mechanisms that we wanted this Club to be run with. And that is, a Manager that plays beautiful football, a Football Director, and a good interaction between them. A strategy of building for the Club, not for the Manager."

As a farewell gift on behalf of Sheikh Mansour, Al Mubarak presented Pellegrini, who has a keen interest in art, with a painting by the late Manchester icon and Manchester City fan, L.S. Lowry, and a second painting by the contemporary Manchester-based artist, Stephen Campbell.

"Pellegrini worked perfectly within the system we were trying to create," continues Al Mubarak, "because he understood and respected the role of the Football Director. He came in with a philosophy of playing football that is the same philosophy that we wanted to bring into the club. An attacking type of football. Beautiful football. A lot of goals. Success. And, at the same time, he understood that he was working within a Club, and that means that as a Manager, you come in with your staff, but you also respect the institution of the Club, and for the first time we were doing that."

CHAPTER 21:

THE CHAIRMAN

By the time Khaldoon Al Mubarak was appointed Chairman of Manchester City in 2008, the statesmanlike 33-year-old already had an enviable CV. He was CEO of the Abu Dhabi Government-owned investment company, Mubadala. He was Chairman [think 'Minister' or 'Secretary'] of Abu Dhabi's Executive Affairs Authority. He was Chairman of more than five companies spanning a diverse range of industries and on the boards of at least eight more.

He was also, and continues to be, a trusted advisor to some of the most senior officials in Abu Dhabi and the UAE, including His Highness Sheikh Mohamed bin Zayed Al Nahyan, the Crown Prince of Abu Dhabi and Deputy Supreme Commander of the UAE Armed Forces [an elder brother of Sheikh Mansour].

However, one thing Al Mubarak had never done was run a football club.

"Honestly, it had never crossed my mind," he says. "I mean, there's many things that you might think through and imagine, but that's really something that I had never thought about."

He pauses for a moment, as if double-checking his memory.

"Never," he says.

He wouldn't get much of a honeymoon period. ADUG's imperious arrival onto the global stage meant that the first-time club Chairman would be thrown straight into the deep end.

"I was just getting my bearings on this," he says, when asked how he felt about taking on the high-profile position. "At the beginning I was just thinking, 'We need to make sure we get the best possible outcome for Sheikh Mansour on this,' because this already was taking on a much bigger size than any of us anticipated. So really, my initial feeling was more on the defensive side, which was, 'We've got to get this one right. We've got to make sure this is in the right place, and whatever that takes, I'll do it.'"

It was only after the initial spike of media interest had subsided, and ADUG's acquisition of 90 per cent of the Club was completed on 23 September 2008, that the Chairman began to think more proactively about the nature of the role he had just taken on, and how he might approach it.

"When I first got into the job, I got a lot of advice from other Chairmen that I know," says Al Mubarak, who even back then thought nothing of picking up the phone to other club bosses around the world to pick their brains. "You have a wide range of types of Chairman. You have Chairmen like Florentino Pérez at Real Madrid, as an example, who are very hands on, and feel that they should be the one to make the decisions on players, build the team, and decide what's in the Club's best long-term interests."

According to Al Mubarak, a long-term student of the game even before he became involved in it professionally, this kind of top-down approach has historically been common in Spain and Italy.

"I remember meeting with the Chairman of Napoli, [Aurelio] de Laurentiis, who gave me similar advice," he says. "Again, very similar approach. He runs the show. He's effectively the Chairman, CEO and Football Director. So, in football you have a lot of that. You had [Massimo] Moratti, in the good old days at Inter Milan. You had [Silvio] Berlusconi in his heyday at AC Milan, where again, he was pretty much the Chairman, CEO and everything. So, you have this 'micro chairman,' I would call it, which is one model."

It isn't everybody's cup of tea.

"In the UK and in the Premier League it seems different," says Al Mubarak. "You have a lot of Chairmen that are very hands-off. Almost the opposite extreme. Here, you had the model which was successful in the 90's and the early 2000's with, let's say two examples, which were Alex Ferguson at Manchester United and Arsène Wenger at Arsenal, where the Chairman was in some ways a figurehead, and the Manager in these cases ran the show. That has kind of evolved at Arsenal since they brought in Ivan Gazidis as CEO [in 2008], but for many years, it seemed like those Chairmen were relatively detached and probably in more of an advisory role."

These two models – both of which have been shown to produce results under the right circumstances – represented vastly different approaches to running a football club. Al Mubarak also consulted around this time with Joan Laporta, then President of FC Barcelona, and David Dein, the former Vice Chairman of Arsenal FC, both of whom he remains in contact with to this day.

"So, obviously I'm talking to all these people," says Al Mubarak, "and I had to figure out, what do I want to be?"

In the end, he says, he didn't adopt any one of these existing approaches in its entirety.

"To be honest, I think I've kind of found my own space here, where my definition of being a Chairman, and what I try to do myself, is to make sure that everybody has a job. The Manager, his job is to win games and run the football team. The Football Director's job is to think about the squad, plan for the future, work out the requirements, and really be the one making those decisions. It's in coordination with everyone, but he's the man when it comes to players coming in and out. The CEO runs the company. He's responsible for the P&L. He's responsible for the human capital side of it. He's responsible for the execution of the overall vision and strategy."

And the Chairman?

"I've always seen the role of the Chairman as the person behind the scenes that enables this orchestra to work," he says. "I think the role of the Chairman is to set a clear vision and strategy, to oversee its execution, and to make sure that there is fluidity and cohesion between all of these other positions. The Chairman sets the vision and the direction, and makes sure that everything is working as it should, but they do not encroach on the responsibilities of the others. That's kind of how I've defined my job over the years."

Despite these self-imposed guardrails, Al Mubarak says there are still situations that call for him to intervene directly in the day-to-day affairs of the Club.

"I've always had this rule," he says, "that the Manager's the Manager, the CEO is the CEO, the Football Director is the Football Director, and the Chairman's the Chairman. Everybody's got their job, everybody's got their responsibility, and everybody's got to respect each other's scope of work."

"However," he continues, "we are in the business of football, and we are in the business of winning, and we are in the business of passion, and sometimes there are instances where you've just got to scrap all that and you need to step in and make a statement, because the team needs something extra. Now what that extra thing is can be intangible. I can't tell you today the next time that I would do it, or why I would do it. You just have to have that sense. But, every time that I have decided to speak to the players, or speak to the organisation, I've done it because I've had a sense myself that I think I need to say something, and that they need to hear it now, or the Manager has come and asked me to do it, and that's happened too."

"The Chairman has given some very important talks to the squad," confirms Brian Kidd, who has served as an assistant coach to the last three Managers at Manchester City. "When things have not been going well, or we might have been going through not the best of times, and he has come in and spoken, it has been inspiring. And I am not saying he makes a massive scene and a song and dance. No, he goes in, to the point, concise. I think he's done no more than four or five, maybe six little talks to the squad, and they have always been inspiring and uplifting."

"He's very straight forward in what he says, and he doesn't go around in circles," agrees Vincent Kompany, "but he's always doing it in a tone where he sounds fair, and he sounds logical and reasonable."

As a senior player and captain, Kompany could be forgiven for being protective of the dressing room environment. However, he says the Chairman's interventions have always been welcome.

"Whenever he's done it, he's made a lot of people's work easier, maybe without even realising it," he says. "Especially for me as the captain, if he comes down in a moment of trouble, a lot of the things he'll say, I might have said it already, or the Manager might have tried to do that, but when the boss comes down and relays a simple and clear message, it kind of nails it down. Then, everybody will abide by these things that might have already been put on the table, but were not being applied, because it's a group, because it's young people, because life is not perfect. In that moment, everybody's back in line, and it gives you a window of time to get down to business."

Al Mubarak says he has no intention of making a habit out of it.

"For it to be impactful, it cannot be common or normal," he says, of his occasional team talks. "It's not something I do weekly, or monthly, or even annually. It's just on those occasions that I feel, or the people that I work with and trust feel, that it's needed. You have to have the trust of the Managers too, because it can be an awkward thing for a Manager to ask from the Chairman. You need to have a high level of trust in that relationship, and luckily I've had that. I have it with Pep for sure, I had it with Pellegrini, and I actually had it with Mancini too."

Despite having a clear vision for how he wanted to approach the role, and some core principles that he intended to apply as Chairman, Al Mubarak says nothing could have prepared him for the reality of actually doing the job.

"I didn't know it was going to be as demanding as it is," he says, despite coming into it with a wealth of experience gained at the highest levels of business and government. "I mean, if you asked me, if we went back to that time, did I anticipate it was going to be as demanding and as consuming as it is? I really didn't anticipate that. It's a lot of energy that you have to put into this, and it's a lot of focus, and I think that caught me off guard."

Al Mubarak insists he isn't complaining.

"It's definitely one of those jobs where you enjoy doing it," he says. "It's not a burden. I enjoy it. The good times, the bad times, and the hard times, but it's not easy. It's non-stop. You're living a season every day, and that can be challenging."

Al Mubarak says that after almost a decade in the chair, he can handle the weekly ups and downs better than he did at the beginning.

"In the early years, if we lost any game, I was unbearable," he says with a laugh. "So, the day we lost, the night we lost, the next day, I would really suffer. And, as a result, my loved ones and the people that I'm comfortable showing my emotions to would have to suffer with me for that 24 hours."

It doesn't sound like fun.

"You should ask my wife," he deadpans.

Al Mubarak says it wasn't sustainable. For anybody.

"Over the years, I've evolved out of that," he says, "and I would say that I am far more mature about it than I was in the early years. So, if we lose now, okay, I'll be upset, but within an hour I'm fine. It used to take me 24 hours at least. Now, I can handle it in a much less emotional way. I can handle the ups and downs better. That's one of the areas where I would say I've evolved the most in the last ten years from being involved in this."

Old habits die hard though, he says, especially around big games.

"I mean, losing a normal game is one thing," admits Al Mubarak, "but last year [2016-17], when we lost to Monaco in the Round of 16? That was a big blow. It took me two or three days to recover from that one. Other than that, though, no, I'm fine!"

Al Mubarak stresses that he isn't arguing for the eradication of emotion from the game. He's just saying that those entrusted with the running of a club need to learn how to keep it in check.

"You cannot be a fan," he says. "Not that passion and emotion aren't important. They're absolutely important. I think it would be criminal to run a sports business and not be emotionally attached, and not be passionate about the sport, and not be passionate about winning and losing. Don't get me wrong. That's crucial. The chemistry of success requires that, in my view."

"Where it's a problem," he continues, "is if it crosses the line and your decision-making becomes emotional and fan-based. And what do I mean by fan-based? Well, after every game, there are emotions that come in, and particularly after losses. There is always that emotional reaction of, 'Well, let's fire the Manager. This player can never play again. We need to change x. We need to change y.' There is always a reaction which, if uncontrolled, could be so dangerous and detrimental to the success of a sports business."

Al Mubarak says that in this aspect of the job, like in so many others, he takes his cues from Sheikh Mansour, the owner of Manchester City and CFG.

"I would say Sheikh Mansour has two incredible assets, among many," explains Al

Mubarak, who knows him best among City officials. "The first one is that he's an athlete, and because he's an athlete, he understands sports. You know, sometimes you win, sometimes you lose, and when you lose there is always another day. Sport is a very emotional business, and if you are emotional, you will suffer, and you will overreact. He is not emotional, and he's not reactive. He's extremely sensible. And it's easy in the good times, when you're winning and having great results. Where that feature is critical, is in the tough times. When you've lost. And Sheikh Mansour has that. He doesn't put extra pressure on a loss or win, because he's always looking at the bigger picture."

"The second advantage," continues Al Mubarak, "is that he's a businessman, and he's very ambitious, and because of that, he's got that entrepreneurial spirit. He took it from his father [the late Sheikh Zayed bin Sultan Al Nahyan, Former Ruler of Abu Dhabi and Founding President of the United Arab Emirates]. He took it from his brother [Sheikh Mohamed bin Zayed Al Nahyan, the Crown Prince of Abu Dhabi]. So, what we've been doing is actually reflective of his attitude in life. We couldn't possibly grow the way we've grown, and do what we're doing, if he didn't have that ambition and entrepreneurial spirit. The fact that he's supported and endorsed this vision to get us to where we are today, just shows you what kind of businessman he is. He has that vision, and it wouldn't work without that."

Sheikh Mansour appears to place a lot of faith in the Chairman's judgement. However, Al Mubarak rejects any suggestion that the owner is in any way detached from the organisation.

"Sheikh Mansour likes to be fully aware of everything to do with Manchester City," he says firmly. "It's his passion. This is really his baby. He wants it to be run efficiently, and effectively, and he has a very clear vision and strategy for where he sees Manchester City and City Football Group going. He's the owner. I give him the facts. I give him recommendations on an objective basis, and he's always made sensible decisions. He's aware of most issues pertaining to the Club in an amount of detail that is quite deep."

One thing that some people find hard to understand is why, after a decade as the owner of Manchester City, Sheikh Mansour has attended only one game in person [a 3-0 win over Liverpool in 2010]. He has reportedly watched the rest on television.

"You know, I want to disconnect these two things," says Al Mubarak. "I want to disconnect his passion and love for the Club, and his being in attendance at games. You have to understand that from his perspective, these things are disconnected. He is fully committed. He is fully impassioned. Every time you see him, it's not hard to feel it."

"But," says Al Mubarak, "he loves this Club in his own way, and within his own environment. Ultimately, I think that going and sitting in the stands and watching it there is just not his style."

Al Mubarak hesitates.

"I don't know if 'style' is the right word to use," he says, without proffering an alternative. "He enjoys it in his environment. But you know, I'm not exaggerating. In ten years, he hasn't missed a single game. I can't remember a game, be it a Premier League game, a Champions League game, an FA cup game, a Capital One or Carabao Cup game, there isn't one of them in the last ten years. He's seen every single one. Even games that are not aired on television, they will find ways for him to see them. So, that's why I want to split these two things."

Al Mubarak knows it can be hard for people to understand. However, he seems perplexed as to why it should bother them. He definitely seems to think it is misinterpreted.

"I get it," he says, "because I'm so close to him, but it's not that he doesn't want to, or that it's a lack of commitment."

Al Mubarak pauses again.

"It's just not his style," he says definitively.

One consequence of the owner's low profile nature is that the Chairman has almost certainly become the most prominent face of ADUG around the world. That has meant that no matter where Al Mubarak goes, and in what capacity, there is one topic that comes up more than any other.

"It is unlike anything else I am involved in," he says. "The whole world is watching this, and when your team is in the Premier League, it's not like you're just dealing with fans in Manchester or in England. You're dealing with the whole world. You're dealing with that guy you meet in the airport in Buenos Aires, to the taxi driver in

Singapore, to every person I bump into between leaving my house and making it to the office in Abu Dhabi every day! It's something that everybody follows, every day, and it's non-stop. And if you win, everybody's got a smile, and if you lose, everybody wants to give you advice or give you criticisms."

Al Mubarak laughs.

"It's constant," he says, without a hint of frustration. "It's non-stop."

He might be the Chairman, but in the world of football, every armchair contains an expert.

CHAPTER 22:

VERSION 19

The City Football Academy [CFA], Manchester, officially opened on 8 December 2014. First conceived as an ambitious idea in late 2008, within months of ADUG's acquisition of Manchester City, the design and construction of the 80-acre facility was a six-year, £200m project from start to finish.

"The design exercise probably took about 18 months and the building that you're sitting in today is built on design version 19," says Jon Stemp, who led the monumental project. "So, we went through 19 design evolutions, constantly challenging whether we needed the space, and whether we were being efficient and respectful of the money we had to spend, and trying to get greater value for money while also protecting functionality, and design version 19 was the one we went with."

The CFA is a work of athletic infrastructural art. It contains 16.5 football pitches, world-class medical and sports science facilities, a 7,000-capacity stadium for women's and youth matches, and on-site accommodation for more than 50 players, coaches and visitors. It incorporates the latest thinking in terms of training, development, treatment, rehabilitation and performance. However, conversations with City officials suggest that the biggest benefit of the CFA is more mundane than that. In short, it has brought all of the Club's employees onto a single site, with football visible from almost every window.

According to Garry Cook, the CEO of Manchester City during the conception and design of the unique facility, creating that purpose-driven sense of place was always at the heart of the plan.

"Phil Knight [co-founder of Nike] always used to say, 'A great brand has a great place,'" recalls Cook, a former Nike executive, "and I said, 'What do you mean by that?' and he said, 'Well, look at our campus [in Portland, Oregon]. It is a great place. It embodies the culture of who we are, and why we live, and why we operate. That is our place. Nobody else can have our place because it is the Nike campus. They can build their own campus and their brand can have their place, but nobody can have this place.' It always stuck with me and I thought, 'Wow, that is powerful.'"

The CFA is unequivocally Manchester City's place. Today, it is also the global headquarters of CFG, which didn't even exist when the original designs for the CFA were being drawn up in 2011.

"It is mind-blowing," says Tom Glick, interviewed in the 'Firsts' meeting room at CFG's HQ building, which overlooks three training pitches and offers a picture postcard view of the nearby first team building. "This is actually my favourite spot in the CFA. There are lots of great spots, but this is my favourite, because it gives you the best perspective of everything. I love that we are surrounded by what we do, we are surrounded by football. There is no way that you can spend a day in this facility, or even a couple of hours, and forget what business we are in."

According to Brian Marwood, who had significant input into the design of the facility from a football perspective, the unification of the sporting and non-sporting parts of the organisation has been transformative.

"We were on three sites previously, so it was very difficult to work how we wanted to work," he says. "We had Platt Lane which was the Academy, Carrington which was the first team, and the Stadium which was the general business, and it was really difficult to get a sense of belonging. There was just such a divide between football and non-football because they never really saw each other, other than on match days."

Now, they see each other all the time. In the cafeteria – dubbed 'Heart of the City' – on the ground floor of the CFA's HQ building, 'the suits' and 'the tracksuits' are now getting their milk out of the same fridge.

"It is kind of inspiring," says Marwood, gesturing out of a meeting room window to where two teams of youth players are engaged in a practice match below. "If you look at this pitch that we are looking at now, primarily since we have been on this site, the 18's have trained there, and because of the configuration of this building, a lot of the staff can watch them play. They could still be working, but watching them train. It is interesting for the staff, but even for the 18's, they know, 'The eyes of the business are on me. I'd better make a good pass here, or I'd better make a good shot, or I'd better run a little bit harder.' There's a little bit of an ego thing there as well. I do think that people feel more connected."

Marwood says that the broad range of teams using the CFA, including playing competitive matches in the Academy Stadium, also sends an important message to the organisation.

"Knowing that we have disability football training here on a Monday night, knowing that the community can use the facility, knowing that the under 18's are there, knowing that the first team are there, knowing that the women's team are over there," he says. "To capture those different communities and have people here watching all of that, the diversity of that alone is powerful."

The most visible forms of community access to the CFA occur via the 32-year old community program, City in the Community [CITC], which has regular access to a wide range of facilities on the site, including a blue all-weather community pitch.

"It was kind of agreed at the initial stages [of the CFA project] that there would be a commitment of 40 hours for community usage of the site every single week of the year, and that was a fantastic commitment," says Mike Green, Head of CITC. "I think we probably use nearer to 60 hours a week. We deliver BTEC [Business and Technology Education Council] programmes here. We deliver disability football programmes here. We deliver free football provision here. There's loads we do, and we couldn't do a lot of it without this."

According to Sir Howard Bernstein, the former Chief Executive of Manchester City Council and now an advisor to ADUG, the CFA is also having an outward impact on the social and economic fabric of East Manchester.

"We have transformed this area," says Bernstein. "More people live here, more people work here, and more people are employed locally by the football club. East Manchester, which was the epitome of Manchester's industrial past and the legacy of industrial dereliction, is now a hub of buzzing activity. More people have access to high-quality community facilities, aspiration has improved, educational standards are improving, and people want to live here now, whereas, 20 years ago or more, people only lived here because they had no choice."

According to Pete Bradshaw, Manchester City's Director of Infrastructure & Estates, the CFA's impact on the local landscape has been aided by its design.

"If we had just put big walls and fences around the place and not cared about what the edges looked like, we would not have had that relationship with the estate," says Bradshaw. "We didn't have to build a wildlife corridor around the site, but it is a better site because we have done that. The site is more valuable because we have done that, the neighbourhood has changed because we have done that, and more people are investing in East Manchester because we have done that."

Even before it opened, the construction of the CFA also included ambitious targets for local procurement and the employment of local residents. According to an independent analysis of the project's economic impact conducted by New Economy in 2015, over 60% of construction jobs for the CFA project went to Greater Manchester residents.[22]

Since its opening, the facility has become a huge draw for football talent from around the world.

"The best people at what they do in the football business want to come and work and live in that place," says Stemp. "So, now we've gone from just taking the existing workforce and giving them the tools to be better at what they do, to actually creating a honeypot for the world's best talent to want to come and be here. The CFA has had a profound impact on our recruitment strategy for players, coaches, and the best football talent on the planet."

"It is unbelievable," says Manchester City's Football Director, Txiki Begiristain. "It makes a difference. It is one of the key things that helps us bring players, and keep players. For me, this is the way that the ownership is showing that they love the game, they love the city and they love the club. They did not need to do that."

"It's been extremely useful to my career," confirms Vincent Kompany, who says it took the first team around three to four months to properly settle into the new facility after moving in. "On top of quality staff, there's so much equipment available to recover properly, to come back from injuries and maintain a level of fitness that's far above what you could do if the only thing you had at your disposal was a football pitch. At my age [32], it's perfect because I can keep in top condition without necessarily having the strain of the old-school plodding that you can sometimes see at other clubs. That is a big reason why everything coming together this way has been perfect for me, because it's allowed me to have more longevity."

"If you want to be a professional footballer, there's just no other place you would go," says England and Manchester City women's captain, Steph Houghton, interviewed on-site at the CFA. "Our training pitches are unbelievable, they get so well looked after. Being able to walk out to five, six or seven thousand fans in games and knowing that you're playing in a half-decent stadium. We've got ice baths, we've got an unbelievable gym, a physio room, pilates room, the food that we get, just all aspects are really covered. The ability to be able to come over here and do this interview in this room, where at other clubs they're probably just doing it in a Costa Coffee shop. So, I think for a professional footballer, male or female, coming to this environment you've got everything you need to try and make it. Then it's probably just down to attitude and mentality to try and utilise everything that we have here."

It is reasonable to ask whether the quality of the CFA's facilities could make players too comfortable. Can a 'No Excuses' environment inadvertently produce a 'No Hardship' experience? This seems especially germane at youth level, where for many of Manchester City's Academy players, the luxurious surrounds of the CFA are the only elite training facility they've ever known.

"I came here once and the first team bus was parked outside the Academy," recalls Jason Wilcox, the former England international and Academy Director at Manchester City. "I said, 'Are the first team here?' They said, 'No, the U-9s are travelling to Leeds for a futsal tournament.' I said, 'What, on the first team bus?' They said 'Yeah,' and I asked, 'How many players?', because futsal is four, and they said, 'Nine players.'"

Wilcox was stunned.

"I said, 'So, we've got nine players under nine, travelling to a futsal tournament in Leeds on the first team bus?!'"

It hasn't happened since.

"The rest of the staff and I have eradicated these things," says Wilcox. "We've said there are going to be certain step changes in our programme to develop more resilience in the players. They're going to have to suffer setbacks. We call them 'bumps in the road.' They have to be left out every now and then. They have to go through times where they're not playing very well and they have to find solutions to things, rather than us always having to find the solution for them."

Begiristain says the same is true at senior men's level, but says that's no reason to forego the best facilities and equipment available.

"There is a risk," he says, "but that is one of the reasons why it helps as well to send some players to other countries. For example, we send players to Girona, and they have new facilities there now, but before, they were training on a pitch that was not the right size. So, yes, we need to show them reality, but we cannot blame the facility. It is up to the people who are running the facility. They are the ones that have to make the players see real life. It does not mean that we do not have to provide them with the best nutritionists, the best physios, the best fitness coaches, the best football coaches."

Steph Houghton says individual players are ultimately responsible for maintaining their own work ethic.

"I've seen players where I think, 'Yeah, they're gonna be good, they're gonna make it,'" she says, "and then potentially because it does become too easy, they stop doing the simple things and stop doing the basics. However, I think the likes of me, Jill [Scott] and KB [Karen Bardsley] have come from a generation where you probably had to fight for everything that you've got, and now we're in this environment, you grab it with both hands."

Away from the training pitch, the CFA has also become a magnet for other types of professionals.

"It's a great working environment," says Tom Glick, CFG's Chief Commercial Officer. "People want to come and work here, so I think it helps us to recruit and retain people. There are so many advantages, but working in sport is a bit of a lifestyle thing, and like in any business, it is good to have a nice place to go to work. This is an extraordinary place to go to work that constantly reminds us of the great business that we are in. It's also a contrast, in a good way, to some of the other places that we have to work around the world."

"It is important across all of the different areas of what we do," says Omar Berrada, Chief Operating Officer of Manchester City. "When I talk to the commercial team now, I say, 'Forget about the PowerPoint presentation. Just bring people here,' because there's no better evidence than actually seeing this. Seeing all the kids – boys and girls – playing football on 16 different pitches, seeing the facilities that we've developed for our Academy and our first team, seeing the Academy Stadium and the investments that we've made at the Etihad Stadium. All of these things are a testament to everything that we've been saying for the last few years, and proof that we mean what we say."

However, Berrada argues that the CFA does more than create a good impression. He says it delivers a range of tangible benefits to the organisation.

"I think it helps enormously on the commercial side," he says, "and for the Academy, if you're a parent and you see these facilities, where else are you going to want to take your kids? Then, on the first team side, Pep [Guardiola] has said publicly, multiple times, that these are the best facilities that he's ever worked at. For me, I think it's one of the main reasons why Pep has decided to extend his contract with us [in May 2018], because he feels so comfortable working in this environment. Finally, for the players, this is amazing because it helps their performance, as individuals and as a team. So, in many ways it's our main selling proposition on both the football side and the commercial side."

According to Stemp, one of the most valuable features of design version 19 has turned out to be its versatility, considering the unexpected demands that have been placed on it in the four years since it opened.

"It is best explained by the fact that when we finished the design, we had 12 teams who were going to occupy the facility," he says. "You go look now and there are 24 teams in this building. I think it's a credit to the design and the innovation of the team behind it that we have doubled the size of the business, in terms of the number of teams, without having to fundamentally change the structure of the building. Now, the question is, did anybody know in 2012 that we were going to have six teams around the world?"

The answer is 'No.' However, it didn't take long for at least two of those clubs – Melbourne and New York – to get their own smaller-scale City Football Academies. According to Stemp, these two satellite facilities are based on the same principles as the CFA in Manchester, and the learnings that have been gleaned from the design, construction and use of that original facility.

"We've kept all of the insights, ideas and intellectual property, and what we've learned since 2008," says Stemp. "We've kept those things alive, and we've scaled them and stretched them and changed them again, and built suitable academies in Melbourne [opened February 2015] and New York [opened April 2018], and we will continue to develop more in other places. You take the basic learnings and principles, then you tweak and change and evolve them, but I think it is a testament to the core principles that we established in Manchester that we can take this knowledge now and reapply it at our other City clubs and make it work."

Although he wasn't there to witness its completion, Manchester City's former CEO Garry Cook takes some muted pride in the CFA, which was largely planned and approved during his time at the Club. He still keeps an A3-sized book that was prepared to celebrate the opening of the facility, a copy of which was sent to him by Stemp in 2014 with a handwritten note, beside the fireplace in his office.

"It may sound over the top," says Cook, "but it really has changed the world of sport."

It has undoubtedly changed the face of East Manchester. However, Cook suggests that without the unique combination of assets that Manchester City, ADUG and Manchester City Council were able to bring to the table, the model would be difficult to replicate elsewhere.

"It was a perfect storm," he says. "The right people came together with the right vision and went on to create something truly special. There were so many reasons why it couldn't be done at the time, but we decided to do it anyway, and now it's something that all of Manchester can be proud of."

CHAPTER 23:

BEAUTIFUL FOOTBALL

Ferran Soriano talks a lot about "beautiful football." Until recently, the phrase was emblazoned on the wall of the ground floor of the CFA's HQ building, as the first and foremost of CFG's three founding principles [along with Football Citizenship and A Global Approach].

"This is entertainment," says Soriano. "It is entertainment with drama and tribalism. That's what football is. So, you can focus on the drama and the tribalism, and forget about the entertainment, and some teams do that. There are coaches that say the important thing is to win, and it does not matter whether you do it beautifully by attacking and scoring, or just defending well. It's just about winning and defending your tribe."

CFG doesn't see it this way.

"There is another way of looking at this that says the product is important. You have to win in style if you can. You have to deliver something that is aesthetically attractive, that entertains people and shows the abilities of the players. This is where we are. We want to win but we want to do it in style. We want to attack and score goals. That is why we ask everybody in the Group to play beautiful football and to keep these pillars for how the game should be played in mind. We actually have an algorithm that defines what beautiful football is, but ultimately it comes down to the show that we offer to the fans."

According to Chairman, Khaldoon Al Mubarak, there are both technical and aesthetic reasons for CFG's ambition for Manchester City and its sister clubs to play a consistently attractive style of football.

"So, I would say the foundation of that is, number one, we want to win, and we have a belief that this is the system that actually gets you the most chances of success in the modern game," he says. "Second, we want to play an attacking type of football, because an attacking type of football is attractive for the fans, it's attractive for viewership, it's attractive for the clubs, and it helps us grow our fan base. We're also all fans of the game ourselves, and we therefore want to be part of something that is good to watch. And third, having that consistent style, and working with coaches that fit within that system, enables us to build a shared philosophy within CFG."

Al Mubarak argues that an 'every manager for himself' approach would be detrimental to the project as a whole.

"If we have a way of playing that changes with every manager, and that's different at every one of our clubs, then I think we lose the whole point of the Group," he says. "The idea of CFG is to create an intellectual property that we can maximise for everyone, but that doesn't work if everyone's going to do their own thing. We need to have a base, and that's where this comes from. It's that base that we think is the right recipe for success, and that everybody can work on in their own way, and that we can use as a foundation at every one of our academies."

According to Brian Marwood, establishing a consistent playing philosophy for Manchester City was one of the first things he was tasked with when he joined the Club in 2009. It was also one of the key planks of the Academy Development Plan approved by the board in 2011.

"We wanted to create a DNA within the Club," he says. "We wanted something that could be referenced. Something that we could all go back to at any point in time and say, 'This is the City spirit, these are the City values, this is the way City plays,' and we wanted to document that."

Marwood says that back then, although the Club had a rich history, it didn't really have a style of play that it could call its own.

"One of the things I always remember asking myself when I came here," he explains, "was, 'What does City stand for? If you close your eyes and think of Man City, what kind of football do you think of?' Back in 2009, there was nothing. I didn't have a reference point. I did with Man United, Barcelona and Ajax. I had a vision of them when I closed my eyes, but I didn't here. So, we wanted to create something that was true to us."

The process began with a series of simple questions.

"There was a group of us that were sat in a room," recalls Marwood, "like the old Liverpool boot room, and we were kind of saying 'How do we want to play? What do we want to be? What are we? What do we want to be known for?' And then you start scoping it out in terms of the profile of players you need, and the manager. There were a lot of references to [Pep] Guardiola in those early days."

Nine years later, Marwood says that, at least from his perspective, the Club has largely succeeded in that effort.

"Now if I close my eyes and I think of Man City, I am thinking of really good football," he says. "I am thinking of 4-3-3, I am thinking of playing through the lines, comfortable playing out from the back. I can see it. Then when I open my eyes, I see it in the first team, I see it with the under 23's, I see it with the Academy teams, I see it in Melbourne, I see it in New York. I can see that it's kind of who we are now."

"I've been here for five years now," says Jason Wilcox, who joined the Academy as a coach in 2013 and became Academy Director in mid-2017, "and the growth of the football methodology is something that I'm really fortunate to have been involved in. We were having methodology meetings every week where we had a group of staff, coaches, and people who played the game, really thinking a lot about our identity and our philosophy. Then we just continued to build on it, and put different layers on, because we all kept growing and looking for the next bit."

It isn't all about the players. Marwood says it is imperative that CFG's coaches understand the methodology and believe in it too, since they are the ones instilling it in their players every day.

"We have got a coaching community that's probably around about 1,000 coaches," he says, referring to the entire CFG network. "We have got to give them that knowledge, we have got to develop them, we have got to find ways to create disciples that are as passionate as we are about the type of football that we want to play."

According to senior City officials, including Al Mubarak, Soriano, Begiristain and Marwood, preserving and advancing the Club's playing philosophy was one of the key drivers behind the appointment of Manchester City's last two first team Managers [Pellegrini and Guardiola].

"What we always said was that we wanted to be Club-led, not Manager-led," says Marwood. "So, the Club would lead the philosophy, and we would appoint a coach to that philosophy. Most clubs tend to just appoint managers, but they can have very different philosophies. In my view, that can lead to inconsistency. We didn't want to do that. We wanted to build something that was consistent, but would keep evolving, and would hopefully enable us to win and play beautiful football. If we can do those two things together, that is utopia."

Manchester City's Football Director, Txiki Begiristain, agrees that the style of football coached in the Academy today is broadly consistent with the tactical techniques deployed by the Club's first team in competitions such as the Premier League and the UEFA Champions League.

"Even before Pep came, the Academy was already playing with the system that we wanted," he says. "They were already starting it. The principles were the same. The 4-3-3. The high pressure. They were already doing it, but now it is almost perfect. Everybody is playing the same system as the first team."

However, Begiristain concedes that not all strategic changes made at first team level will necessarily filter down into the Academy, because its primary focus is player development.

"The first team is a reference," he says. "We play 4-3-3, but if we have a specific goal and it needs to change, it changes. We cannot always make those changes when we are developing players [in the Academy]. But, we use the same system, or couple of systems, and they are all based on the same principles."

Wilcox says that the Academy's football methodology is not something that can be easily distilled.

"It's very difficult to express it in five minutes," he says. "because I could talk about it all day, every day, and it's difficult to articulate."

However, he agrees to outline it in broad brushstrokes.

"If a goal gets scored after we have possession from the goalkeeper, and the ball goes in the back of the net after 33 seconds, I get as much pleasure from the first second as the 33rd," he says. "So, it's the build-up to the goal scoring chance, and the way we have done it, that is my passion. It's not just about getting the ball from the defenders to the strikers as quickly as possible. We have to progress through the pitch together. There are a lot of different concepts within that which are very detailed. Like I say, I can't tell you in a few minutes, but it's about dominating the game through possession. We want to take the ball to the opposition. When we lose possession, it's about regaining it as quickly as possible, and having players regain their natural positions as quickly as possible. It's positional play, so it's about occupying areas of the pitch to gain superiority, and it's just been a fantastic journey."

Beyond the first team and the Academy, the same principles have also been adopted by Manchester City's women's team.

"I think the basic structure is the same as what you would see in any of our teams," says Gavin Makel, Manchester City's Head of Women's Football. "We are easily recognisable as a Manchester City team through the way that we play, with a 4-3-3 system or a variation of that, our wing backs pushing high, combination play, ball possession, and trying to play attacking football."

"It's pretty much the same," says England and Manchester City women's team captain, Steph Houghton. "If you look at Pep's team, if you look at the teams in the Academy, and now even our Centre of Excellence, we're all adapting the same methodology. We want to play attractive football, we want to have the ball, and we want to control games, and I think once you get in a routine and get into good habits then it comes quite naturally."

Houghton says that by now she can instantly spot the methodology when she sees it in action.

"Yeah, definitely," she says. "We watch a lot of the coaching sessions. We watch the lads' games on a Saturday, and even John Stones at the minute for England, you can watch him and think, 'I know exactly what's he's trying to do. He does that for Man City. He's trying to draw someone out so he can play someone else,' and if you're a mad football fan, which I am, not just because I play it, but because I love watching it, you're a little bit of a geek like that, aren't you? You look at the technical side of it, but that's just because every single day, that information's thrown at you in different scenarios on the training pitch."

There may be no going back now, at least for the current generation of City players. According to Begiristain, who was a member of Johan Cruyff's FC Barcelona 'Dream Team' in the 1980's [alongside Pep Guardiola], any strain of possession-based football can quickly become addictive.

"There are other ways to win," says Begiristain. "The problem is that when you win this way once, it is the only way that you want to win. This is what I say to everybody. Once you taste this way, you only want to win this way."

"Why?" he asks, pre-empting the question.

"Because it is not about just scoring one, two or three goals, and you remember the three goals," he says. "You will remember that you are always in the opponent's half. You are dominating. You win the ball back immediately. The attitude of the team is good, they are well-organised with the ball, and everything is almost perfect. Forget about the three-nil, four-nil, four-one, three-one or two-one. It is about watching your team having the ball, all the time, in your opponent's half."

Begiristain contrasts this with other approaches, even those that might deliver the same end result.

"So, if you go back and think, you can win 3-0 again, but this time with only three counterattacks, because you are staying in defence all the time, and the other team has possession," he says.

He holds his palms up.

"It sounds stupid," he says, "but do you want to have the ball, or do you not want to have the ball?"

He doesn't wait for an answer.

"If you can win 3-0, and get the exact same result, I prefer to have the ball," he says. "I prefer to be close to the goal. It sounds so stupid, but once you have experienced that, you do not want to play the other way, even though both ways can win."

Begiristain glances at the magnetic football pitch on his office wall. All of the pieces are in the attacking half.

"It happened to me," he says. "Once you play this way, then you do not want to go back. You always want to do that."

CHAPTER 24:

WATCHING FROM THE WINGS

Mike Summerbee played on the right wing for Manchester City from 1965 to 1975. He won four trophies at the Club from 1968 to 1970, scoring in the 4-3 win over Newcastle that clinched the 1967-68 League title, and setting up the winning goal in the 1969 FA Cup Final. The England international and Manchester City legend was made an official Ambassador of the Club in 2009, one year after the ADUG takeover.

Txiki Begiristain played on the left wing for FC Barcelona from 1988 to 1995. The Spain international won nine trophies as a player at the Camp Nou, including four La Liga titles in a row from 1990-91 to 1993-94. He was appointed Football Director at Manchester City in November 2012, where he would eventually reunite with his former FC Barcelona teammate and colleague, Pep Guardiola, in 2016.

Brian Marwood played on the left wing for Sheffield Wednesday from 1984 to 1988 and at Arsenal from 1988 to 1990, where he won a League title in 1988-89. He played one match for England in 1988, joined Manchester City as its Chief Football Administration Officer in 2009, and is now CFG's Managing Director of Global Football.

From their privileged vantage points at Manchester City, these three former wingers all agree that they have never seen anything quite like the football played by the Club under Pep Guardiola in 2017-18.

"This is a revolution in football in this country," says Summerbee. "Every other football club is trying to play the same as what we do now. Pep comes from the [Johan] Cruyff era – and I played against Cruyff – and Pep has a way of playing that a lot of other people are trying to play like, but you have to have the players who can do what he wants to do. Last season [2017-18], some of the opposing fans would stay in the ground after games to clap our team off the field, because they've never seen football like it."

Begiristain agrees, and says that although the Club could still be recruiting well and winning games without Guardiola, they couldn't produce this particular brand of football without him.

"No, not the same," he says. "Playing good football for sure, but not the same football, and not the same way. I think Pep takes this team, and any team, to another level. It is difficult, because it is not only Pep, because other teams are winning, right? But, I am saying that to play this football, Pep is the best in the world by far."

When asked about Manchester City's initial and ultimately unsuccessful outreach to Guardiola back in 2013, and whether the Club would have been ready for him back then, Begiristain is in no doubt.

"Yeah, of course," he says. "Any club is ready for Pep. It should be ready and if it is not, he makes you ready immediately because of his intensity, his passion, and the rhythm of everything. He is so intense that he makes everybody the same, and that makes everything go faster."

"Oh, yeah," says Marwood, when asked if the Club is finally playing the kind of football that he and his colleagues dreamed about nine years ago when they first set out to create a distinctive playing philosophy for Manchester City. "This is the best and, not being disrespectful to Manuel [Pellegrini], to Roberto [Mancini] or to Mark Hughes, but this is the best football by a country mile, not just for this football club, but that I have seen in my time in football. It's just this level of quality, this level of talent, this ability to move the ball around in these intricate patterns that cut through teams. Amazing goals that involve a fantastic amount of passes. It's entertainment. It is pure entertainment."

"Sometimes when we play now it takes your breath away," says Summerbee, "especially when you watch some of these players like David Silva. I don't want to name individual players, but David Silva is a magician. He's amazing, but every player has contributed, and that's why it's a team game. Everybody's got a job to do, whether they can pass a ball 25 yards, whether they can beat two or three people, and that's what makes a team successful, when everybody's working for each other and they've all got an ability to do something for the side."

People often struggle to articulate just what it is that makes Guardiola and his teams so effective and captivating to watch. That might be because it isn't just one thing.

"The most important part of the setup is the goalkeeper," says Summerbee. "The goalkeeper has the confidence that spreads throughout the side. He's great on the ball. He can pass the ball. Everything starts from the back and they work it and do it that way. Then there's the possession of the ball. Sometimes you see opposing sides, they come and make a defensive situation of putting everyone behind the ball, and you'll just see us passing the ball and passing the ball, and then it's like opening a safe, where suddenly they create that opening. I've never seen that before."

Summerbee says that while it couldn't be done without the right players, Guardiola's ability to harness the talent he has at his disposal should not be underestimated.

"Pep is creating something special, and you've got to have the players with the confidence to play that way," he acknowledges, "but he creates that confidence, not only in the players and the team, but in the football club itself. I watch him at training and they work on situations where they have control of the ball, everybody from the goalkeeper to [Sergio] Agüero, to Leroy [Sané] and others. They can all pass the ball and control the ball with confidence. Everybody."

"If he's got weaknesses, I've not seen them yet," says captain, Vincent Kompany. "It's more of a style that he embeds rather than regimented principles, if you know what I mean? It's obviously offensive and free flowing football, but it's almost like geometry. The positions that we have to take, the relationships, there's not one player that can move without causing something else to move elsewhere, which was never the case in any of the teams I've played in before."

Kompany says Guardiola brings a unique tactical versatility and strategic intelligence to his craft.

"The team is solid in so many ways, not only its depth in terms of quality, but also its breadth in terms of the different assets that we have," he says. "We can change tactics. We can change so many little concepts within the same framework. And as a teacher, he's by far the best I've had. I think all coaches should be teachers, and he excels in that. He makes a lot of complicated things seem very simple."

For Begiristain, who has already climbed this mountain with Guardiola once before, he's been most struck by the pace of the progression over the last two seasons and how quickly the Manager has adapted to the distinctive challenges of English football.

"You need to change," says Begiristain, who says it took him some time to recalibrate his own thinking to the physical nature of the English game. "You know, coming from Spain, you are more looking for the quality of the player, and here you obviously need the quality – the talent has to be there – but you are also buying energy, strength and size. Football in England, just in my opinion, is influenced a lot by the number of games that you have to play. You play more games than in other countries, so you have to sign players that are more physical. They have to be bigger, because you need the power and the strength to play that number of games."

Begiristain says that the way the game is refereed in England also has an impact on recruitment decisions.

"There is more contact between the players," he says. "In Spain, there might be more quality, but here it is not enough because the big guys, the strong ones, they can play against the small ones because they allow more contact here. For me, when I came, I said, 'Oh my God,' when you go to play at Cardiff, or Stoke, or Crystal Palace, or West Bromwich, some of their players are over 185cm and there's no free kicks, the referees are not giving you anything. So, we had to change."

In simplified terms, that meant injecting more size and strength into key locations on the pitch.

"So, you sign the [Benjamin] Mendy, you sign the [Kyle] Walker, you have [Nicolás] Otamendi, we have [Vincent] Kompany, we have [John] Stones and [Aymeric] La

Porte," he says. "You can still have the smaller guys of course. We have [David] Silva, we have [Raheem] Sterling, we have [Gabriel] Jesus, but you also need the size. So, I changed my mind a little bit, and I think Pep had to change a little bit too, but finally we are coming back to our place again. We have the quality and we have the physicality in the squad. We have almost everything."

Whatever the reason, it is fair to say that Guardiola didn't get off to the greatest start in English football. In 2016-17, his first season in charge, Manchester City finished third in the Premier League, and was knocked out in the semi-finals of the FA Cup, the fourth round of the League Cup, and the Round of 16 in the UEFA Champions League.

Despite coming up empty-handed, Manchester City Chairman, Khaldoon Al Mubarak, maintains that he preached patience at the end of the season. He and others at the Club had waited a long time for Guardiola and their faith in him was not easily shaken.

"He had a very frustrating first year," says Al Mubarak. "That was very tough on him professionally, but he came back strong. I always believed in him, even when we weren't getting the results."

The Chairman knows some people will dismiss this as 20/20 hindsight.

"It's easy to say it now, after the season we had this year [2017-18]," he concedes, "but I'm telling you. I genuinely believed that first year. I wasn't upset. I wasn't too irritated. As frustrating as it was, and as disappointed as I was with the results, because they didn't reflect where we were supposed to be at, I could see that we were on to something that just needed a bit more patience. I kept telling Pep, 'It's going to happen. It's going to take whatever it's going to take in terms of time, but I can see clearly where we're going. I can see the success that's going to come. Just keep doing what you're doing. It is going to click.' I could see it, and it happened."

In the 2017-18 season, Manchester City dominated the Premier League, becoming the first team to accrue 100 points in a season in the history of the competition. The Club also set new records for the number of goals scored [106], the number of games won [32], the longest winning streak [18 games], the number of successful passes in a single game [942], and the most possession recorded in a single game [82.95%]. The final winning margin of 19 points [ahead of second-placed Manchester United] and goal difference [+97] were also Premier League records.

In a nostalgic tribute to 'Typical City,' the champions only secured their hundredth point courtesy of a last-minute Gabriel Jesus goal in the last game of the season [a 1-0 win over Southhampton] on 13 May 2018.

In May 2018, Pep Guardiola signed a two-year contract extension at Manchester City that will keep him at the Club until the end of the 2020-21 season. Al Mubarak says that Guardiola's greatest achievements at Manchester City may ultimately come in the achievements of others.

"His ability to improve players is his strongest feat, and that's a tangible thing," he says. "You can look at many cases within the team, players that we've brought in, and you can see how much they have evolved and improved under Pep. He's really made everybody a lot better. He's a winner. He's a serial winner. He knows how to win, and he knows what it takes to win."

Summerbee agrees that Guardiola is a master at getting the most out of his players, both as individuals and as a group.

"People think the hardest part is getting there," he says. "The hardest part is staying there. You know, week in, week out, making sure your manager can rely upon you, doing what he wants you to do. You might not play as well some games but as long as your work rate's there, and your enthusiasm is there, that's what it is all about, and Pep's got that with his players. He's got the respect of the players. They work hard and they know what they've got to do."

Summerbee then says something unexpected.

"The only regret I've got in my lifetime is that he was never my manager," he says, "because I would have liked to have played under him."

This warrants interrogation.

"It's the way that he plays," explains Summerbee. "It's about possession of the ball. Keeping the ball and creating situations. Playing with width and attacking with pace. I used to play as a winger, and sometimes centre-forward, and it would suit me, you know? If the ball is on one side, and I'm over here, I could get the ball and it's a one-to-one situation."

There are generations of Manchester City fans that would have loved to have seen that. However, as much as he'd liked to have played under Guardiola, 75-year-old

Summerbee insists he really is content to sit back and watch the show – most of the time.

"I don't miss playing football, because I had it all my life," he says. "My father played football as well, so it is a family thing, but I don't miss it at all, except when there's a game on because I want to kick the ball."

Summerbee says he might not be the only one holding back that particular urge on match days.

"You see Pep," he says with a laugh. "The only thing he doesn't do is play. If he got to the touchline he'd play you know, and that's it. That's what it's all about."

CHAPTER 25:

THE GAME

If there is one word that people at Manchester City use more than any other to describe Manager Pep Guardiola, it is 'intense.' After that comes 'detailed,' and both are intended as compliments.

"I love my job," says Guardiola, intensely fiddling with a plastic bottle cap on his desk while he talks in his office in the CFA's first team building. "I am a Latin guy. I express my feelings, so people know exactly how I feel just by looking at my face. It's easy to understand me. I love my job, I put all of myself into it, and I try to do my best. I don't want to lose."

Contrary to popular opinion, Guardiola says there are no aesthetic motivations behind the beautiful football that his teams have become known for producing throughout his career as a manager.

"No, no, I want to win," he says. "That phrase, 'beautiful football,' I don't use that. Never. So, I want to win, but from my experience, the best way, and the way I believe brings us closest to winning, is the way we play. We want to express ourselves, and sometimes when it happens, it is attractive for the people that are watching, but to play in that way, you need talented players. Without that, it's not possible to achieve what we achieved. So, we need quality, but what I want is to win."

It is hard to believe that there is no artistic strand to the way Guardiola thinks about the game, but he is emphatic about it, pointing to the defensive records of his teams throughout his career as evidence that he doesn't prize attacking flair over other equally important aspects of the game.

"No, no, no," he says. "I'm not romantic or aesthetic. So, in the period since 2008 or 2009, always our teams were the best defensive team in the league. Just one season we were not the best. And for that, you have to work a lot defensively, but when you talk about beautiful football, you are not talking about this kind of thing – the defence, being aggressive without the ball, how you can let them run, or not allow them to run, you know?"

Rather than beauty, Guardiola says his philosophy is inspired by what originally sparked his players' love for the game: the ball.

"The way we want to play," he explains, "with the ball, is because I believe that all of the players decided once in their life, when they were kids playing football, that they enjoyed playing with the ball. The reason why is the ball. So, when people ask, 'What is your philosophy?', or 'What are you going to do?', it's the ball. They decided to play, and I want to let them express themselves in that way, but of course, it's not only that. You have to have ideas, and everybody has to follow, because it's a team, and you need to do extra things – in defence, with the ball, without the ball – but always focused on the ball. That is what we want."

Although Guardiola's players spent a lot of time with the ball in his first year at Manchester City [2016-17], the end results fell short of expectations, with a third-place finish in the Premier League the pinnacle of the team's achievements.

"It was the first time I did not win one title in a season," he says, "and the expectation was so high. We didn't accomplish our goals, and always you reflect. The Manager is always revaluating day-by-day. What is going on? What has happened? Are we going in the right direction, or do you have to change something? But, I felt the Club, not just Khaldoon of course, because he's the Chairman, but the people here, Txiki, the staff, all the people who surround me, said 'It's okay. It's going to be well.' I didn't feel anything was wrong. No. We understood it was part of the process. So, sometimes you [snaps fingers] get it quicker, sometimes you need more time."

Guardiola says there wasn't a moment when he knew things had turned around. He says it doesn't work like that. However, he suggests the renewal of the squad had a big impact.

"No, there is not a moment," he says. "Football is not a process like that. It's not a finished business. Always you have to improve, and when you are going well, you cannot be relaxed, because tomorrow you're going to be down, and when you're down, you need to be calm, and try to analyse things, because you're going to be up again. Of course, in the middle of the first season, we realised that we were clearly an old team. Magnificent players, but we were an old team, that lacked a little bit of energy, and that's why we invested last season [2017-18]. This season [2018-19] we're going to invest less. Much, much less. We are going to refresh the team. That was the main reason for the success of last season, and now we need to have continuity, and consistency, for the next time."

On transfer business, Guardiola relies on two of his closest confidantes, CEO Ferran Soriano, and Football Director, Txiki Begiristain, both of whom he worked with at FC Barcelona, and who were instrumental in bringing him to Manchester City. He has also developed a close relationship with the Manchester City Chairman, Khaldoon Al Mubarak, over the last two-and-a-half years, which both describe independently as a genuine friendship.

Soriano says Guardiola has changed in subtle ways since they last worked together and seems more patient. Guardiola agrees.

"I think I have changed more than them," says Guardiola, of his compatriot colleagues, "because when I started to work with them, I was in my first or second season as a manager, and my energy, and my perspective on situations, was different. Before, I wanted things [snaps fingers] right now, right now, right now. I want a player, right now, tomorrow he has to be here. I want to sell a player, tomorrow. I want to have a training session, right now. It was age, you know? Now, I am more understanding of situations. They are the same nice guys."

After a slow start, CFG's faith in Guardiola was quickly repaid with a record-breaking 2017-18 season in which Manchester City won the League Cup and the Premier League, and became the first team in the history of the competition to accrue 100 points in a season. However, Guardiola says the many titles he has won aren't something he spends a lot of time thinking about.

"Normally, the trophies only count to give you more time to continue to work, and to express more of your ideas," he says. "Titles help you to win time. Time to keep going if you want to stay. But, a title for itself?"

Guardiola seems sceptical of the value of that. In fact, there are no trophies in his office.

"No, no," he says. "I'm not a guy who looks at the curriculum vitae, and says, 'Oh, how many seasons have I won?' That doesn't make me happy. I'm not the guy who goes to... I don't know, the bank... to see how many I have."

For Guardiola, he seems to be in it more for the stimulation of the contest, and the timeless challenge of developing winning strategies and then coaching and cajoling his players to execute them to perfection on game days.

"That is the reason why we are managers," he says. "The relations, the convincing them, the seducing them, the tactics we want to play, the way we want to play. I am a manager for that – for the tactics, for understanding the game. It is chess."

Guardiola then picks up speed.

"They do this, I want to do that," he explains feverishly. "I know they want to do that, I have these players, and they can make it tricky to beat them on the right today, now the left. We can make this movement to help with the other one - "

The imaginary tactical scenarios unfolding in Guardiola's mind cease as quickly as they began.

"It's a game," he says simply. "The word 'game' explains everything. When we were little boys, a game is what we wanted. To play something. It's the same."

Some of this can be hard to reconcile. One moment, Guardiola says he is driven only by the desire to win. Minutes later, he appears enthralled by the complexities of the game itself, and committed to deepening his understanding of it. He's intensely competitive, but says the titles and trophies are immaterial to him, and he forgets about them soon after they've been won. However, upon closer inspection, the apparent contradictions in Guardiola's way of thinking are not necessarily contradictions at all. Ultimately, what he seems to be saying is that he loves the game, intensely and in detail, and the objective of the game is to win.

"The important thing is the process," he says. "How we do what we do to win. That is the key point. What we do in our relations with others, how we live every single day in the locker room, our relations with other human beings in the training session, how we respect our opponents, the way we want to play. That is where it is nice to build something. To achieve. Of course, we are so happy when we win, and especially because of how happy we make our families, the fans, and other people. Trophies also help to make the brand, Manchester City, stronger around the world, and that is so important for stability. It is important for the players. A lot of players hadn't won anything, and we were able to win the Premier League. It was amazing for me too. It was a dream to win the Premier League, but after two or three weeks, I say, 'Okay, now we are thinking about the next one.' That's life. That's sport. It isn't about just winning one title. Many people do that in their career. The difference is the way we did it, and how consistently we can do it in the future."

There's an old saying in golf, 'It's not how, it's how many.' Guardiola, an avid golfer himself, appears to believe the opposite when it comes to football. It is actually all about the 'how,' as long as you win in the process. That's the game.

CHAPTER 26:

UNFINISHED BUSINESS

In the summer of 2017, with two years remaining on his current contract at Manchester City, captain Vincent Kompany sat down with his wife, Carla, to write a list of every football trophy he could potentially win before the end of the 2018-19 season.

"There was something like 12 trophies I could win before the end of my contract, and we literally set the target on every single one of them," he says. "Everything I can have, I want to have it with City."

Apart from the Premier League and the League Cup [which Manchester City won both of in 2017-18], Kompany's list also included the FIFA World Cup [his Belgian side finished 3rd], and two shots at the UEFA Champions League. The competition, arguably the most prestigious in club football, remains the biggest piece of unfinished business in the resurgence of Manchester City since 2008.

The first of those two chances dissolved in April 2018, when Manchester City went down to Liverpool in the quarter-finals, leaving just one more UEFA Champions League campaign on the captain's list in 2018-19.

"It was disappointing this year to go out to Liverpool, and the situation around that game, particularly the way the team was treated going into the stadium [at Anfield on 4 April 2018], didn't make for a nice atmosphere that night," says Brian

Marwood. "And obviously, we lost to Real Madrid the last time we got to the semi-finals [2015-16], but we didn't really turn up for that game. It kind of feels like we're building towards this now though, and Pep's got great experience and great knowledge when it comes to winning Champions Leagues, but I think the hard part is that the English Premier League is such a demanding league."

This is a common refrain from City officials. The view, shared by other English clubs, is that it is more difficult for Premier League sides to compete at the pointy end of the UEFA Champions League because they have such a grueling schedule to contend with at home during the knock-out phase of the competition.

Brian Kidd, who won a European Cup at 19 with Manchester United in 1968, played for Manchester City in the UEFA Cup in the late 1970's, and has been an assistant coach to the last three Managers at Manchester City, agrees that English sides have it tough competing in Europe in the sense that they can never afford to take their eye off the ball at home.

"I think the Premier League is the most demanding league in Europe for obvious reasons," he says. "You do not get a winter break, and you cannot take anything lightly. If you are not at it you will get beat by the bottom team. The top team can easily get beat by the bottom team. If you are not concentrating, you do not work harder, and you do not run harder, you can get beat."

In the last seven years, Manchester City has made the semi-finals once [in 2015-16 under Pellegrini], the quarter-finals once [in 2017-18 under Guardiola], the Round of 16 three times [in 2013-14 and 2014-15 under Pellegrini, and 2016-17 under Guardiola], and was once knocked out twice in the group stage [in 2011-12 and 2012-13 under Mancini]. The only English side to win the competition in the last ten seasons was Chelsea FC in 2011-12, and they finished 6th that year in the Premier League.

Manchester City's women's team, which has won the FA Women's Super League [2016], FA Women's Cup [2017] and two FA WSL Continental Tyres Cups [2014, 2016] since 2014, faces similar obstacles in its bid to take out the UEFA Women's Champions League. Compounding matters in the women's game, English sides are generally fielding salary capped squads against European rivals that aren't subject to the same limitations in their home competitions. Manchester City have made the semi-finals of the UEFA Women's Champions League twice in the last two years and been knocked out both times.

"God, I've been in, how many semi-finals now?" asks captain, Steph Houghton. "Five semi-finals, for both Arsenal and Man City, so it's like, 'Okay, there's got to be one where we're going to make a final.' But, to make the semi-finals in the last two years has been a great achievement for us, considering we've got a lack of experience in that competition. It's definitely the pinnacle of club football for any footballer, so, I think it's something that for me personally, and I'm sure if you spoke to Nick [Cushing, Manager] and the rest of the girls, it's something that we want. We want to try and get to the final, and we want to try and win it."

ADUG officials have made no secret of the fact that winning the UEFA Champions League is high on their list of targets for Manchester City.

"The only thing we didn't do this year is really move forward significantly in the Champions League," says Chairman, Khaldoon Al Mubarak. "And ultimately, if you want that stamp of global recognition, it means winning the Champions League, and we're still not there yet. However, I think we're certainly on our way."

"We have now won the Premier League three times since 2012," says Manchester City board member, Simon Pearce. "We have won numerous cups, and we have come second [in 2012-13 and 2014-15]. That is working, and we know we are winning or coming in the top four every year. That machine is doing what it is supposed to, and we know the questions to ask and the things we need to do to keep that happening. There is one thing that is not happening that needs to be repetitively occurring, and that is winning or at least competing for the Champions League. That is the challenge. The machine is not quite tweaked like a Formula 1 car, and this thing needs to be doing 90,000 RPM to get to the outcome we want."

However, those that have been involved in successful UEFA Champions League campaigns at other clubs say it's important to keep in mind the nature of the competition, because there is only so much that each club can control.

"Of course, everybody wants it," says Manager, Pep Guardiola. "We want it as well, but you know, knockout games can depend on many things. In the Premier League it's 38 games, so the best and most consistent team always wins. But in the Champions League, it's [snaps fingers], a bad ten minutes, a bad decision, and you are not able to win. I think that sooner or later, it's going to happen. But, to win the Champions League you have to win more Premier Leagues in a row, or be in it for more time, so that when you travel to Europe, the people, the referees as well, and everybody, thinks, 'Okay, that club is good.' That is the first thing. The second thing is to be always there, always there, always there. So, I think the target is to win Premier Leagues as much as possible over the next five or ten years, and arrive always in the quarter-finals of the Champions League, then one day arrive in the semi-finals, and when you do this, one day you will get it."

"It is important," agrees Manchester City CEO, Ferran Soriano, "but it should not be an obsession, because winning the Champions League involves talent, ability and competitiveness, but also luck. That is the reality because of how the competition is organised. It is like the World Cup. So, it is important because it would be a signal that the club is at the top of the top, but we cannot be obsessed with that, because we might do very, very well, but not win the Champions League for ten years, and that is okay. For example, Real Madrid, who I am mentioning because they have won the last three, went through two periods in their history where they probably had the best team in Europe, but never won the Champions League."

"Barcelona is a top team," adds Guardiola. "You cannot deny that. But its first Champions League was in '92, and they missed three or four [European Cup] finals before that, so they were fighting for the title for 40 years before they were able to do that!"

At 32 years of age, Vincent Kompany doesn't have ten years to wait. He certainly doesn't have 40. While he's still got his boots on, the Manchester City captain is determined to grab every piece of silverware he can, and few titles are as tantalising and elusive as the UEFA Champions League.

"It's a lifetime dream for us," says Kompany. "As kids, we grew up and we looked at this, and we could never even imagine putting our hands on these kinds of trophies. It's also such a competitive environment, with top players, people that we know, people that you know, the clubs and everything behind them. To actually have a chance to be one of those very few chosen ones, it's one in how many? There's 400 million people that play football in the world. 400 million. So, what are the odds of winning what everyone wants? You're competing all your life to even get to that stage, then you're competing again to win the trophies, and these chances don't come often."

For Kompany, who signed with Manchester City shortly before the ADUG takeover in 2008, and has been an iconic presence at the Club over the last ten years, it's clear that each additional title means more to him than just another notch on his belt.

"To be able to do something good in sports, which is so volatile, shows that you're able to be part of something special," he says. "You're excelling, and you can change people's lives as well. You can do so many things in this world, but to how many people does it genuinely matter? How much recognition will you get for it, anyway? And even if you do something that matters, you might not get the recognition for it. But, if you win trophies with a football club, for that period of time, you're on top of the world. And then..."

Kompany snaps his fingers.

"...it goes again," he says sadly, "but it's worth everything to just experience it even once in a lifetime."

CHAPTER 27:

PATIENCE AND AGGRESSION

With the benefit of hindsight, it was perhaps inevitable that His Highness Sheikh Mansour bin Zayed Al Nahyan would one day become the owner of a Premier League football club.

"I have always enjoyed business, I have a love for the game, and I like to compete," he says simply, 10 years after becoming the owner of Manchester City. "Investing in a club was an obvious thing to do."

That part may have been obvious to him. In 2008 though, luckless Manchester City was not an obvious choice to many.

"The challenge was finding the right club," admits Sheikh Mansour. "For me, it had to be in the Premier League, and the fundamentals of the organisation had to be right in order for there to be potential to compete at the highest level. It couldn't be about becoming involved in a club that just made up the numbers."

Despite the hardships that Manchester City and its supporters had endured over the preceding three decades, or perhaps because of them, Sheikh Mansour says he was confident that the 114-year-old Club was built on solid foundations.

"The fundamentals of City are unshakable," he says. "They had been tested with the team's fall to the lower division and were obviously strong. City was everything I was looking for. It was a sleeping giant."

It's fair to say that 'sleeping' is a generous description of Manchester City in 2008, with ADUG's due diligence process revealing a Club that was virtually in a coma after years of underinvestment.

"I would say that its potential most definitely outweighed its assets," says Sheikh Mansour, diplomatically, "but that's what I was looking for and the sale price reflected that."

Recognising the scale and complexity of the transformation project that lay ahead, Sheikh Mansour needed to put somebody in charge of the process that he could trust. For that, he turned to Khaldoon Al Mubarak, an emerging figure in business and government circles in the UAE, and a personal friend that Sheikh Mansour knew shared his love for football.

"Khaldoon is someone I know very well," he says. "We both share a passion for the game and as I looked at potential clubs to invest in, I spoke with him and got his views. The conversation about him becoming Chairman was a natural next step."

It doesn't sound like it was a long conversation though, with Sheikh Mansour's initial instructions to the Chairman short enough to fit inside a fortune cookie.

"The mission has always been simple," he says. "Become the best club in the world both on and off the field."

Over the last ten years, the two have collaborated closely on the oversight of Manchester City and now CFG.

"He and I speak about City almost daily," says Sheikh Mansour.

He stops and rethinks this.

"No. Actually pretty much daily," he says. "I think we have the ideal understanding and working rhythm. It allows me to be involved as much or as little as my schedule will allow. He knows what I need to know and what I like to know and what I have time to know. They are rarely the same thing."

Although he has only attended one match in person at the Etihad Stadium in the last ten years, Sheikh Mansour repeats the Chairman's assertion that he never misses a game, describing them as a "circuit breaker" in his busy life.

"I love watching the games," he says. "That's ultimately what is most important.

At the end of the day, I am a fan of the Club and live the games in the same way as every other fan. I watch the games at home or wherever I am in the world. Sometimes that can be pretty challenging, but we always find a way."

As the owner of the Club, he thinks it might sometimes be easier for him to see the silver lining in matches that don't end up going City's way, since he views each game as part of a longer-term process.

"Matches are proof of life for me of where we are in our progress," he explains. "We have lost many games over the years that have been real indicators of positive change. So, whilst I haven't liked the result, I have felt positively about our greater progress. That's an upside of being in my position."

However, some games clearly have more riding on them than others, and Sheikh Mansour says the FA Cup semi-final win over Manchester United on 16 April 2011 was a watershed moment in Manchester City's journey over the last 10 years.

"That was the moment I knew we had arrived at a new level in our climb to where we wanted to be," he says, vividly recalling the contest. "The team was deliberate in its performance that day. After the semi-final I was convinced that we were in the right place to win the final. I don't think I ever felt nervous, simply because the team were playing with the right mentality."

Sheikh Mansour says he was just as stunned as anybody else when Manchester City won its first Premier League title a year later on 13 May 2012, but that this had more to do with the way that it happened, rather than any great surprise over the fact that the Club had won the League.

"The QPR game for me was exactly as it was for everyone else. I don't think we will ever see anything like that again," he says. "Winning the League was an incredibly important moment, but one we had planned and worked hard for. My hope is that we compete for the Premier League every year, so it was a feeling that I knew we had to get used to quickly."

It was shortly after that first title win that Manchester City's Chairman, Khaldoon Al Mubarak, and the Club's board and new CEO, Ferran Soriano, proposed an unexpected diversion from the linear – albeit accelerated – rebuilding strategy that had been pursued up to that point.

Sheikh Mansour says he didn't hesitate when presented with the opportunity to create City Football Group, and to establish a new club in New York City, but refutes any suggestion that the decision was made lightly.

"The team didn't bring me a concept," he says firmly. "They brought me a well thought out plan, so it was very easy to see how robust the proposition was. It all made absolute sense at the time. It still makes absolute sense."

The sale of 13% of CFG to a consortium of Chinese investors for US$400m in 2015, in a deal that valued the Group at US$3bn, provided a degree of vindication for that decision, not to mention the accelerated investment that was made into Manchester City in the early years of the ADUG ownership.

"In my experience, a lot of potential investment returns get wasted when there is too great a focus on immediate financial outcomes," says Sheikh Mansour. "You can be patient and aggressive at the same time, and build real momentum behind an organisation so that it strengthens and delivers continuously over the medium and longer terms. We had done that and the sale of the 13% [of CFG] was proof that we had built the value we intended to build. The funding has allowed us to invest and build even more value. The investment was good for CFG for that reason, and because China will always be important for Manchester City and CFG."

What's not yet clear is where the project ends. While many predicted Sheikh Mansour would get bored and abandon Manchester City once the novelty of owning a Premier League club wore off, this particular investor shows no signs of losing interest any time soon. In fact, he makes no attempt to disguise the fact that he fully intends to move the goalposts.

"The journey for City was always about trying to complete our work in a way that saw us achieve benchmarks that had yet to be set within football," he explains. "To do that we had to look at everything and make sure that every part of the organisation, and what it did, moved to a new standard for football. We're not there yet, but we have come a long way. And I think people who know me well will tell you that if we ever do look like we are getting there, we will set new standards and targets to aim for."

Although he might sound hard to please in business, Sheikh Mansour the football fan seems more than satisfied with the football being played by Manchester City a decade after he bought the Club.

"Beautiful, intelligent and passionate," he says, when asked to describe the way the team played under Pep Guardiola in 2017-18. "It's the kind of evolved game that I had hoped we would one day achieve."

CHAPTER 28:

KILLING THE GAME

Historian Gary James left Manchester City in January 2009, just four months after the ADUG takeover. His museum at the stadium closed down shortly after.

"I had stayed longer than I should have done really," says James, looking back on that period of his life, "but I was passionate about the museum. It had won awards and delivered quite a lot. It brought an average of about 24,000 people to the Stadium each year, which at the time was equivalent to a League Cup game. So, I was proud of that, but I probably should have gone before 2008, because the constant negativity at the Club around that time was wearying."

Some people attributed James's departure to a falling out with then CEO, Garry Cook, or a philosophical objection to the ADUG ownership and its plans for the Club. James says neither was the case.

"I think people thought that I had left because I did not share the vision, but it was the absolute opposite," he says. "I wanted to be part of this new City, but I was frustrated with people, some of whom were in fairly senior positions, who did not share that vision themselves, and I was a small cog, so I left. I actually felt for Garry Cook and the others that were coming in to try and change things."

These days, James regularly returns to Manchester City as a football historian and as a fan. A season ticket holder for the last 30 years, when he walks through the gates of the CFA, or watches games from the North Stand of the 55,000-seat Etihad Stadium today, he says it is impossible not to notice how much has changed at the Club in the last ten years. However, in the long arc of Manchester City's history, James says the seismic transformation under ADUG has actually brought the Club closer to its traditional position in English football than many people realise.

"It sounds bizarre, but I think it is more like City than it was," he says. "Manchester City had major trophy success earlier than Manchester United, 26 years before Arsenal, and 51 years before Chelsea, and won a major European trophy before Liverpool. My first proper memory of anything at City was Rodney Marsh signing in 1972, when I was four or five, and he was one of the biggest names in football at the time. Then, in the late 70's, Kaziu Deyna arrived from Poland, from behind the Iron Curtain. I was only 10 or whatever, and I do not even think I knew what the Iron Curtain was, but he came from behind it to play for City, and that was the most exotic thing on the planet. So, the City of the 70's liked to bring in superstars. Often we failed. I mean Kaziu Deyna was too slow by the time he got here. But that was the City that I knew as a child, and the City that I see now is that plus so much more."

James says that even the tactical sophistication of the Guardiola era echoes earlier periods in the Club's history.

"Manchester City were tactical innovators in the 1950's," says James, before recounting the story of then Manager Les McDowall's use of the tactical system known as the Revie Plan, which took the Club to two consecutive FA Cup Finals in 1955 [lost] and 1956 [won].

"Malcolm Allison in the late 60's and early 70's was a coaching genius and he tried to introduce different tactical innovations too," says James. "City once had a reputation for trying to do stuff that was a little bit different. So, what Pep is doing now fits with that tradition of the Club, and as a fan I just cannot wait for next season."

James appreciates that not everybody sees it that way.

"I am 50, and a lot of fans of my age and above get a bit negative talking about modern football. They say things like, 'Well, the success is great but it is not the same atmosphere,' or, 'It is not the same team spirit,' or, 'It is not like this or that.'"

"I disagree," says James. "For my daughter, who is now 21, this is everything it was to me in the 70's. Everything. For her, the atmosphere is fantastic. It's a different atmosphere to the 70's, but I lived through the 80's where you would go to football matches and be scared that a dart or a sharpened coin would be thrown at you from the other side of the fence. That's how it was."

"Now, I am sat there in a beautiful blue stadium watching a team of talented players," he says. "Players like Vincent Kompany might not be from Manchester, but they are acting more Mancunian than players from a few years back. He gets it. He understands what the club is. Pablo Zabaleta did too."

In James's estimation, they aren't the only ones.

"The players, the manager, the directors, they all seem to have a shared view of what this football club should be, and I sort of wish, not entirely, but to some extent, I wish that we could eradicate the period from 1995 to 2005, or even 2008, because that is the period that for me was out of keeping with City's history. That is the period where we had lost our way. We used to say things like 'This Is Our City,' and 'Pride in Battle,' all those sorts of sayings, but did we actually believe it?"

James has his doubts.

"Now, in this stadium, we do not need to say those things," he says. "It is around us."

Khaldoon Al Mubarak couldn't agree more. For all of the investments that ADUG has made in infrastructure and personnel over the last ten years, he says that eradicating the pervasive negativity that had taken up residence at the Club in the 25 years prior to the takeover might yet prove to be the most powerful legacy of this important decade in the history of Manchester City.

"I want to distinguish between two things," says Al Mubarak. "I want to distinguish between history on the one hand, and superstition associated with incidents from history on the other. I think history is crucial. This Club has a 125-year history and that's something that we're very proud of, and I'm a big supporter of making sure that history is always part of the story."

Al Mubarak chooses his words carefully.

"However, what I didn't like was the negativity that sometimes came with that. The superstition that something was bound to go wrong, because by the way, that superstition was not 100 years old. I suspect that didn't exist in the early 1900's, or the 1920's or the 1930's, or the 1950's, 60's and 70's, when the Club was successful. That started in the late 70's, the 80's and the 90's, during that period of underachievement, and that's the thing that I've been dead against, because it spills over, and we need the crowd to have a positive energy."

As newcomers to Manchester City, it didn't take Al Mubarak and his colleagues long to feel the weight of low expectations pressing down on their shoulders.

"I struggled in the beginning," he admits, "because this was so heavily ingrained in the fan base, and with people involved with the Club. For the first few years, we had to try and convince people that this was a new Club, it was a new ownership, it was new players. Everything was different, and that 'Typical City' premise based on the last 30 years of history no longer needed to apply."

According to Al Mubarak, the turning point probably came at 93:20 on 13 May 2012, when City overcame QPR in the most improbable of circumstances to win the Club's first League title in 44 years.

"I think that game, and that turnaround, finally started to break that subculture," he says. "And now, you have a new generation coming in. You look at the 10-year-olds, the 15-year-olds, the 17-year-olds, and even the 20-year-olds. They have just lived through the last seven years, when Manchester City has been the most successful Club in the Premier League, and I think that changes the mindset."

After ten years, one FA Cup, three League Cups, and three Premier League titles, a well-founded sense of optimism appears to have taken root at Manchester City.

"I think we have a unique set of circumstances right now," says Al Mubarak. "We have the Club in the right place and on the right trajectory. We have the right Manager, that fits with everything that we're trying to do for this Club. We have the right players. We have the right infrastructure, the right people, and an incredible fan base. Everything is kind of falling into place, and what we saw this year was really the fruits of that."

After scoring 106 goals and collecting 100 points in the 2017-18 Premier League season, the Club that was so often accused of killing the game just a few years ago has even gained some grudging respect from other members of the football community.

"Almost everybody wants to watch Manchester City play," says Al Mubarak. "Not just in England. Globally. I hear it from people all the time. I travel to South East Asia, to South America, to North America, many places in Europe, and people will tell me, 'We love watching Manchester City play. We're fans of Barcelona, or Real Madrid, or Manchester United, or Juventus, or Bayern Munich, but we watch Manchester City,' and I think that's an incredible sign of success."

It's a familiar feeling for Mike Summerbee, whose arrival at Manchester City as an ambitious 23-year-old coincided with the last golden period in the Club's history.

"I've been associated on and off with this club since 1965, so I've seen a vast amount of changes through the years," says Summerbee, "but the situation here now, since Sheikh Mansour's taken over, and our Chairman, Khaldoon Al Mubarak, it's just a completely different world we're living in. It's something that I never thought I'd see in my lifetime."

After sticking with Manchester City through the turbulent ups and downs of the last half century, Summerbee says that nobody deserves the Club's current success more than its loyal fan base.

"The fans have always been there," he says. "They've always been supportive, and for them as well, since day one when the initial takeover happened, their lives have completely changed, and now we've got a club that can compete at the highest level in Europe, and anywhere else you can think of."

Summerbee, who first visited Abu Dhabi to play an exhibition match in 1977, when Al Mubarak was only two years of age, has developed a close relationship with the owner and the Chairman.

"They've been absolutely superb," he says. "I don't care what you say, or what other people say. People are envious of the way this football club is being run. I have never come across anything like it, and I never will again. This football club is in safe hands, and now we're on a journey that will continue well after I've passed away."

It's a morbid thought, but one that leaves Summerbee smiling.

"When I see the Chairman now and I talk to him, he always says to me, 'We've only just started, Mike.'"

ENDNOTES

1   Bhoyrul, Anil, 'Abu Dhabi seals deal to buy Manchester City', Arabian Business, 1 September 2008, https://www.arabianbusiness.com/abu-dhabi-seals-deal-buy-manchester-city-44156.html

2   Ogden, Mark, 'Manchester City v Manchester United: Life president Bernard Halford insists the tide is turning blue,' The Telegraph, 15 April 2011, https://www.telegraph.co.uk/sport/football/teams/manchester-city/8455087/Manchester-City-v-Manchester-United-Life-president-Bernard-Halford-insists-the-tide-is-turning-blue.html

3   Conn, David, 'Richer Than God: Manchester City, Modern Football, and Growing Up,' 2012, Quercus, p.235

4   Brennan, Stuart, 'Roberto Mancini: The man behind Manchester City's greatest-ever season,' 2012, Carlton Books Ltd, p.116

5   Ryan, Mark, 'When you have suffered for a long time you have more passion - that's what Manchester City fans have: The world according to Roberto Mancini,' Daily Mail, 11 September 2010, http://www.dailymail.co.uk/home/moslive/article-1310224/Manchester-City-Roberto-Mancini-When-suffered-long-time-passion--thats-Manchester-City-fans-have.html

6   Taylor, Daniel, 'Roberto Mancini: I like being a manager. I like being angry every day,' The Guardian, 22 February 2013, https://www.theguardian.com/football/2013/feb/22/roberto-mancini-interview-angry-every-day

7   Samuel, Martin, 'Roberto Mancini interview: I came to Manchester City to win - not for the weather!', Daily Mail, 24 September 2010, http://www.dailymail.co.uk/sport/football/article-1314670/Roberto-Mancini-Interview-I-came-Manchester-City-win--weather.html

8   Reade, Brian, 'How Barca reserve Yaya Toure was seduced by the whore of world football,' The Mirror, 9 July 2010, https://www.mirror.co.uk/opinion/football-opinion/brian-reade-column-millions-squandered-3353824

9   Rooney, Wayne, with Allen, Matt, 'My Decade In The Premier League,' HarperSport, 2012, p.227

10 Agüero, Sergio, [written by Frescó, Daniel], 'Born to Rise: My Story,' 2014, Trinity Mirror Sport Media, p.466

11 Agüero, Sergio, [written by Frescó, Daniel], 'Born to Rise: My Story,' 2014, Trinity Mirror Sport Media, p.466

12 Affleck, Kevin, 'Khaldoon Al Mubarak defiant over wantaway Carlos Tevez,' The National, 25 January 2012, https://www.thenational.ae/sport/khaldoon-al-mubarak-defiant-over-wantaway-carlos-tevez-1.372626

13 Ferguson, Alex, My Autobiography, 2013, Hodder & Stoughton, p.312

14 Ferguson, Alex, My Autobiography, 2013, Hodder & Stoughton, pp.303-304

15 Agüero, Sergio, [written by Frescó, Daniel], 'Born to Rise: My Story,' 2014, Trinity Mirror Sport Media, p.17

16 Ferguson, Alex, My Autobiography, 2013, Hodder & Stoughton, p.308

17 Ferguson, Alex, My Autobiography, 2013, Hodder & Stoughton, p.304

18 Soriano, Ferran, 'Goal: The Ball Doesn't Go In By Chance: Management Ideas from the World of Football,' 2011, Palgrave Macmillan

19 Bagli, Charles V. and Belson, Ken, 'A Team Is Born, but Not All Cheer,' The New York Times, 21 May 2013, http://www.nytimes.com/2013/05/22/sports/soccer/manchester-city-and-yankees-to-own-mls-franchise-in-new-york.html

20 Bagchi, Rob, 'Sepp Blatter and Michel Platini banned for eight years by Fifa,' The Telegraph, 21 December 2015, https://www.telegraph.co.uk/sport/football/fifa/12061288/Sepp-Blatter-and-Michel-Platini-banned-for-eight-years-by-Fifa-live.html; Gibson, Owen, 'Michel Platini resigns as Uefa president after ban reduced to four years,' The Guardian, 9 May 2016, https://www.theguardian.com/football/2016/may/09/michel-platini-cas-appeal-ban-football

21 Jackson, Jamie, 'Manuel Pellegrini: If I don't get an interesting offer I will quit football,' The Guardian, 30 May 2016, https://www.theguardian.com/football/2016/may/30/manual-pellegrini-manchester-city-exclusive-interview

22 City Football Group and Manchester City Council, 'City Football Academy Impact Report: Economic impact of investment and development in the City Football Academy and associated developments in East Manchester,' 2016, p.3